PERSONAL INFORMATION

Name: ....

Address: ....

....

Phone: .... Email: ....

Employer: ....

Address: ....

....

Phone: .... Email: ....

MEDICAL INFORMATION

Physician: .... Telephone: ....

Allergies: ....

Medications: ....

Blood Type: ....

Insurer: ....

IN CASE OF EMERGENCY, NOTIFY

Name: ....

Address: ....

Phone: .... Relationship: ....

Moving
Mountains

►►► 2024 Planner ◄◄◄

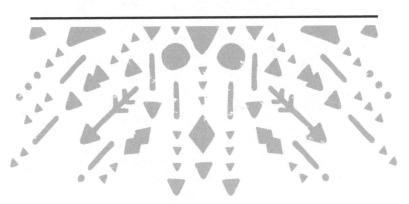

BARBOUR
PUBLISHING

2024 Is Your Year to Move Some Mountains!

"Truly I tell you, if you have faith as small as a mustard seed, you can say to this mountain, 'Move from here to there,' and it will move. Nothing will be impossible for you."

MATTHEW 17:20 NIV

The Bible says that "without *faith* it is impossible to please God" (Hebrews 11:6 NIV, emphasis added). God places faith's importance at the very top of the list, and the reason is simple: it is the key by which we gain access to Him. How can we love Him when we aren't sure He exists? How can we trust Him when we aren't sure He wants to be part of our lives? By faith we come into God's presence and establish a relationship with Him.

Moving Mountains will open your eyes to faith; it will help you take it from word to concept to experience. As you move through the pages of this planner, you will hear God's voice calling you to place your faith in Him in every aspect of your life—each day of 2024 and beyond!

2024

JANUARY

S	M	T	W	T	F	S
	1	2	3	4	5	6
7	8	9	10	11	12	13
14	15	16	17	18	19	20
21	22	23	24	25	26	27
28	29	30	31			

FEBRUARY

S	M	T	W	T	F	S
				1	2	3
4	5	6	7	8	9	10
11	12	13	14	15	16	17
18	19	20	21	22	23	24
25	26	27	28	29		

MAY

S	M	T	W	T	F	S
			1	2	3	4
5	6	7	8	9	10	11
12	13	14	15	16	17	18
19	20	21	22	23	24	25
26	27	28	29	30	31	

JUNE

S	M	T	W	T	F	S
						1
2	3	4	5	6	7	8
9	10	11	12	13	14	15
16	17	18	19	20	21	22
23	24	25	26	27	28	29
30						

SEPTEMBER

S	M	T	W	T	F	S
1	2	3	4	5	6	7
8	9	10	11	12	13	14
15	16	17	18	19	20	21
22	23	24	25	26	27	28
29	30					

OCTOBER

S	M	T	W	T	F	S
		1	2	3	4	5
6	7	8	9	10	11	12
13	14	15	16	17	18	19
20	21	22	23	24	25	26
27	28	29	30	31		

YEAR *at a* GLANCE

MARCH

S	M	T	W	T	F	S
					1	2
3	4	5	6	7	8	9
10	11	12	13	14	15	16
17	18	19	20	21	22	23
24	25	26	27	28	29	30
31						

APRIL

S	M	T	W	T	F	S
	1	2	3	4	5	6
7	8	9	10	11	12	13
14	15	16	17	18	19	20
21	22	23	24	25	26	27
28	29	30				

JULY

S	M	T	W	T	F	S
	1	2	3	4	5	6
7	8	9	10	11	12	13
14	15	16	17	18	19	20
21	22	23	24	25	26	27
28	29	30	31			

AUGUST

S	M	T	W	T	F	S
				1	2	3
4	5	6	7	8	9	10
11	12	13	14	15	16	17
18	19	20	21	22	23	24
25	26	27	28	29	30	31

NOVEMBER

S	M	T	W	T	F	S
					1	2
3	4	5	6	7	8	9
10	11	12	13	14	15	16
17	18	19	20	21	22	23
24	25	26	27	28	29	30

DECEMBER

S	M	T	W	T	F	S
1	2	3	4	5	6	7
8	9	10	11	12	13	14
15	16	17	18	19	20	21
22	23	24	25	26	27	28
29	30	31				

AUGUST 2023

SUNDAY	MONDAY	TUESDAY	WEDNESDAY
30	31	1	2
6	7	8	9
13	14	15	16
20	21	22	23
27	28	29	30

notes

THURSDAY	FRIDAY	SATURDAY
3	4	5
10	11	12
17	18	19
24	25	26
31	1	2

....
....
....
....
....
....
....
....
....
....
....
....

JULY

S	M	T	W	T	F	S
						1
2	3	4	5	7	7	8
9	10	11	12	13	14	15
16	17	18	19	20	21	22
23	24	25	26	27	28	29
30	31					

SEPTEMBER

S	M	T	W	T	F	S
					1	2
3	4	5	6	7	8	9
10	11	12	13	14	15	16
17	18	19	20	21	22	23
24	25	26	27	28	29	30

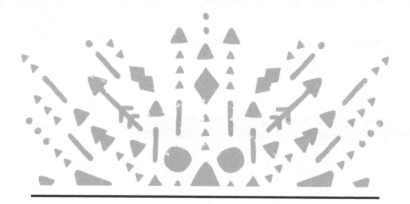

Courageous Footsteps

In Jesus' day, women had fewer opportunities to stretch their wings creatively and professionally than they do today. That didn't stop them from holding tightly to God's promises and stepping out to act on what they believed. You can follow in their courageous footsteps. Whatever you believe God wants you to do, big or small, don't hold back. Today, take at least one step toward your goal. With God's help, you'll accomplish everything He's set out for you to do.

Goals *for the* Month

....
....
....
....
....
....
....
....
....
....
....
....
....
....
....
....

*"Blessed is she who has believed that the
Lord would fulfill his promises to her!"*
LUKE 1:45 NIV

AUGUST
2023

S	M	T	W	T	F	S
		1	2	3	4	5
6	7	8	9	10	11	12
13	14	15	16	17	18	19
20	21	22	23	24	25	26
27	28	29	30	31		

Being rich in faith is the secret to leading an abundant life. That's because faith allows us to see life from God's perspective.

to-do list

- [ ]
- [ ]
- [ ]
- [ ]
- [ ]
- [ ]
- [ ]
- [ ]
- [ ]
- [ ]
- [ ]
- [ ]
- [ ]
- [ ]
- [ ]
- [ ]
- [ ]
- [ ]

SUNDAY, JULY 30

MONDAY, JULY 31

TUESDAY, AUGUST 1

WEDNESDAY, AUGUST 2

THURSDAY, AUGUST 3

FRIDAY, AUGUST 4

SATURDAY, AUGUST 5

to-do list

- [ ]
- [ ]
- [ ]
- [ ]
- [ ]
- [ ]
- [ ]
- [ ]
- [ ]
- [ ]
- [ ]
- [ ]
- [ ]
- [ ]
- [ ]
- [ ]

"I have come that they may have life, and that they may have it more abundantly."

JOHN 10:10 NKJV

AUGUST

2023

S	M	T	W	T	F	S
		1	2	3	4	5
6	7	8	9	10	11	12
13	14	15	16	17	18	19
20	21	22	23	24	25	26
27	28	29	30	31		

God's power is at work behind the scenes. He promises to bring something good out of every situation, no matter how things may look on the outside.

to-do list

☐
☐
☐
☐
☐
☐
☐
☐
☐
☐
☐
☐
☐
☐
☐
☐
☐
☐

SUNDAY, AUGUST 6

MONDAY, AUGUST 7

TUESDAY, AUGUST 8

WEDNESDAY, AUGUST 9

....
....
....
....
....

THURSDAY, AUGUST 10

....
....
....
....
....

FRIDAY, AUGUST 11

....
....
....
....
....

SATURDAY, AUGUST 12

....
....
....
....
....

to-do list

☐
☐
☐
☐
☐
☐
☐
☐
☐
☐
☐
☐
☐
☐
☐
☐
☐

We live by faith,
not by sight.
2 CORINTHIANS 5:7 NIV

AUGUST
2023

S	M	T	W	T	F	S
		1	2	3	4	5
6	7	8	9	10	11	12
13	14	15	16	17	18	19
20	21	22	23	24	25	26
27	28	29	30	31		

Once you put your faith in Jesus, you are assured of spending eternity with Him—that is meant for sharing. Pass it on—and you'll be blessing future generations!

to-do list

- [ ]
- [ ]
- [ ]
- [ ]
- [ ]
- [ ]
- [ ]
- [ ]
- [ ]
- [ ]
- [ ]
- [ ]
- [ ]
- [ ]
- [ ]
- [ ]
- [ ]
- [ ]

SUNDAY, AUGUST 13

MONDAY, AUGUST 14

TUESDAY, AUGUST 15

WEDNESDAY, AUGUST 16

THURSDAY, AUGUST 17

FRIDAY, AUGUST 18

SATURDAY, AUGUST 19

to-do list

- [ ]
- [ ]
- [ ]
- [ ]
- [ ]
- [ ]
- [ ]
- [ ]
- [ ]
- [ ]
- [ ]
- [ ]
- [ ]
- [ ]
- [ ]
- [ ]

*This is the secret:
Christ lives in you. This
gives you assurance
of sharing his glory.*

COLOSSIANS 1:27 NLT

AUGUST
2023

S	M	T	W	T	F	S
		1	2	3	4	5
6	7	8	9	10	11	12
13	14	15	16	17	18	19
20	21	22	23	24	25	26
27	28	29	30	31		

In the Bible, God shares how much He loves you, what He's been up to since the creation of the world, and His plans for the future. You're an important part of those plans!

to-do list

- [ ]
- [ ]
- [ ]
- [ ]
- [ ]
- [ ]
- [ ]
- [ ]
- [ ]
- [ ]
- [ ]
- [ ]
- [ ]
- [ ]
- [ ]
- [ ]
- [ ]
- [ ]

SUNDAY, AUGUST 20

MONDAY, AUGUST 21

TUESDAY, AUGUST 22

WEDNESDAY, AUGUST 23

THURSDAY, AUGUST 24

FRIDAY, AUGUST 25

SATURDAY, AUGUST 26

to-do list

☐
☐
☐
☐
☐
☐
☐
☐
☐
☐
☐
☐
☐
☐

These are written so that you will put your faith in Jesus as the Messiah and the Son of God. If you have faith in him, you will have true life.

JOHN 20:31 CEV

AUGUST
2023

S	M	T	W	T	F	S
		1	2	3	4	5
6	7	8	9	10	11	12
13	14	15	16	17	18	19
20	21	22	23	24	25	26
27	28	29	30	31		

This week, invite God's Spirit to sear the Bible's words into your heart. Then step out in faith and put what you've learned into practice.

to-do list

- ☐
- ☐
- ☐
- ☐
- ☐
- ☐
- ☐
- ☐
- ☐
- ☐
- ☐
- ☐
- ☐
- ☐
- ☐
- ☐
- ☐

SUNDAY, AUGUST 27

MONDAY, AUGUST 28

TUESDAY, AUGUST 29

WEDNESDAY, AUGUST 30

....

....

....

....

....

THURSDAY, AUGUST 31

....

....

....

....

....

FRIDAY, SEPTEMBER 1

....

....

....

....

....

SATURDAY, SEPTEMBER 2

....

....

....

....

....

to-do list

- [ ]
- [ ]
- [ ]
- [ ]
- [ ]
- [ ]
- [ ]
- [ ]
- [ ]
- [ ]
- [ ]
- [ ]
- [ ]
- [ ]
- [ ]

Truth, righteousness, peace, faith, and salvation are more than words. Learn how to apply them. You'll need them throughout your life.

EPHESIANS 6:14–16 MSG

SEPTEMBER 2023

SUNDAY	MONDAY	TUESDAY	WEDNESDAY
27	28	29	30
3	4	5	6
	Labor Day		
10	11	12	13
17	18	19	20
24	25	26	27

THURSDAY	FRIDAY	SATURDAY
31	1	2
7	8	9
14	15	16
21	22	23 *First Day of Autumn*
28	29	30

....
....
....
....
....
....
....
....
....
....
....
....
....
....

AUGUST

S	M	T	W	T	F	S
		1	2	3	4	5
6	7	8	9	10	11	12
13	14	15	16	17	18	19
20	21	22	23	24	25	26
27	28	29	30	31		

OCTOBER

S	M	T	W	T	F	S
1	2	3	4	5	6	7
8	9	10	11	12	13	14
15	16	17	18	19	20	21
22	23	24	25	26	27	28
29	30	31				

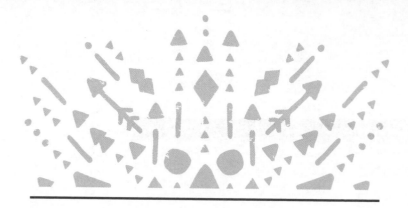

Heart Changes

What you believe will influence the choices you make. If you believe in gravity, you won't jump from a seventh story balcony to save time in getting to your hair appointment. If you believe what Jesus says, you'll change the way you live. Jesus often talks about the importance of traits such as honesty, purity, and generosity. Though God's Spirit helps change your heart, it's the daily choices you make that help bring traits like these to maturity.

Goals *for the* Month

....

....

....

....

....

....

....

....

....

....

....

....

....

....

....

....

....

....

*Jesus went to Galilee preaching the Message
of God: "Time's up! God's kingdom is here.
Change your life and believe the Message."*
MARK 1:14–15 MSG

SEPTEMBER
2023

S	M	T	W	T	F	S
					1	2
3	4	5	6	7	8	9
10	11	12	13	14	15	16
17	18	19	20	21	22	23
24	25	26	27	28	29	30

Blessings are gifts straight from God's hand. The more frequently you thank Him for His blessings, the more aware you'll be of how many more there are to thank Him for.

to-do list

- [ ] ....
- [ ] ....
- [ ] ....
- [ ] ....
- [ ] ....
- [ ] ....
- [ ] ....
- [ ] ....
- [ ] ....
- [ ] ....
- [ ] ....
- [ ] ....
- [ ] ....
- [ ] ....
- [ ] ....
- [ ] ....
- [ ] ....
- [ ] ....

SUNDAY, SEPTEMBER 3

MONDAY, SEPTEMBER 4 *Labor Day*

TUESDAY, SEPTEMBER 5

WEDNESDAY, SEPTEMBER 6

THURSDAY, SEPTEMBER 7

FRIDAY, SEPTEMBER 8

SATURDAY, SEPTEMBER 9

☐
☐
☐
☐
☐
☐
☐
☐
☐
☐
☐
☐
☐
☐

"Turn to face God so he can wipe away your sins, pour out showers of blessing to refresh you, and send you the Messiah he prepared for you, namely, Jesus."

ACTS 3:19–20 MSG

SEPTEMBER
2023

S	M	T	W	T	F	S
					1	2
3	4	5	6	7	8	9
10	11	12	13	14	15	16
17	18	19	20	21	22	23
24	25	26	27	28	29	30

Instead of viewing challenges as negative, faith helps you see them as opportunities for growth. A stronger faith results in a more balanced life.

to-do list

- [ ]
- [ ]
- [ ]
- [ ]
- [ ]
- [ ]
- [ ]
- [ ]
- [ ]
- [ ]
- [ ]
- [ ]
- [ ]
- [ ]
- [ ]
- [ ]
- [ ]
- [ ]

SUNDAY, SEPTEMBER 10

MONDAY, SEPTEMBER 11

TUESDAY, SEPTEMBER 12

WEDNESDAY, SEPTEMBER 13

THURSDAY, SEPTEMBER 14

FRIDAY, SEPTEMBER 15

SATURDAY, SEPTEMBER 16

to-do list

☐
☐
☐
☐
☐
☐
☐
☐
☐
☐
☐
☐
☐
☐

Anyone who meets a testing challenge head-on and manages to stick it out is mighty fortunate. For such persons loyally in love with God, the reward is life and more life.

JAMES 1:12 MSG

SEPTEMBER
2023

S	M	T	W	T	F	S
					1	2
3	4	5	6	7	8	9
10	11	12	13	14	15	16
17	18	19	20	21	22	23
24	25	26	27	28	29	30

Continued growth and change is a joint effort between you and God. If there's any area in your life that seems resistant to change, talk to God about it right now—and every morning until change takes place.

to-do list

- [ ]
- [ ]
- [ ]
- [ ]
- [ ]
- [ ]
- [ ]
- [ ]
- [ ]
- [ ]
- [ ]
- [ ]
- [ ]
- [ ]
- [ ]
- [ ]
- [ ]

SUNDAY, SEPTEMBER 17

MONDAY, SEPTEMBER 18

TUESDAY, SEPTEMBER 19

WEDNESDAY, SEPTEMBER 20

THURSDAY, SEPTEMBER 21

FRIDAY, SEPTEMBER 22

SATURDAY, SEPTEMBER 23   *First Day of Autumn*

to-do list

☐
☐
☐
☐
☐
☐
☐
☐
☐
☐
☐
☐
☐
☐

Don't become so well-adjusted to your culture that you fit into it without even thinking. Instead, fix your attention on God. You'll be changed from the inside out.

ROMANS 12:2 MSG

SEPTEMBER

2023

S	M	T	W	T	F	S
					1	2
3	4	5	6	7	8	9
10	11	12	13	14	15	16
17	18	19	20	21	22	23
24	25	26	27	28	29	30

Life only moves in one direction: forward. Only by letting go of yesterday can you welcome today's opportunities with open arms.

to-do list

- ☐
- ☐
- ☐
- ☐
- ☐
- ☐
- ☐
- ☐
- ☐
- ☐
- ☐
- ☐
- ☐
- ☐
- ☐
- ☐
- ☐
- ☐

SUNDAY, SEPTEMBER 24

MONDAY, SEPTEMBER 25

TUESDAY, SEPTEMBER 26

WEDNESDAY, SEPTEMBER 27

....
....
....
....
....

THURSDAY, SEPTEMBER 28

....
....
....
....
....

FRIDAY, SEPTEMBER 29

....
....
....
....
....

SATURDAY, SEPTEMBER 30

....
....
....
....
....

to-do list

- [ ]
- [ ]
- [ ]
- [ ]
- [ ]
- [ ]
- [ ]
- [ ]
- [ ]
- [ ]
- [ ]
- [ ]
- [ ]
- [ ]
- [ ]
- [ ]
- [ ]

*"Forget the former things;
do not dwell on the past.
See, I am doing a new
thing! Now it springs up;
do you not perceive it?"*

ISAIAH 43:18–19 NIV

OCTOBER 2023

SUNDAY	MONDAY	TUESDAY	WEDNESDAY
1	2	3	4
8	9 *Columbus Day*	10	11
15	16	17	18
22	23	24	25
29	30	31 *Halloween*	1

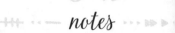

notes

THURSDAY	FRIDAY	SATURDAY
5	6	7
12	13	14
19	20	21
26	27	28
2	3	4

....
....
....
....
....
....
....
....
....
....
....
....
....

SEPTEMBER

S	M	T	W	T	F	S
					1	2
3	4	5	6	7	8	9
10	11	12	13	14	15	16
17	18	19	20	21	22	23
24	25	26	27	28	29	30

NOVEMBER

S	M	T	W	T	F	S
			1	2	3	4
5	6	7	8	9	10	11
12	13	14	15	16	17	18
19	20	21	22	23	24	25
26	27	28	29	30		

Worries into Prayers

Sometimes it feels like it's a woman's job to worry. If you can't be assured that all of your loved ones' physical and emotional needs are being met, fretting about them makes you feel involved—like you're loving them, even if you're powerless to help. But you know someone who *does* have the power to help. Anytime you feel the weight of worry, whether it's over someone else's problems or your own, let faith relieve you of the burden. Turn your worries into prayers.

Goals *for the* Month

....
....
....
....
....
....
....
....
....
....
....
....
....
....
....

Don't fret or worry. Instead of worrying, pray.
Let petitions and praises shape your worries
into prayers, letting God know your concerns.
PHILIPPIANS 4:6 MSG

OCTOBER
2023

S	M	T	W	T	F	S
1	2	3	4	5	6	7
8	9	10	11	12	13	14
15	16	17	18	19	20	21
22	23	24	25	26	27	28
29	30	31				

When you spend time together, you pick up the habits of the people you're with. In the same way, the more time you spend with God, the more your character begins to resemble His.

to-do list

- [ ]
- [ ]
- [ ]
- [ ]
- [ ]
- [ ]
- [ ]
- [ ]
- [ ]
- [ ]
- [ ]
- [ ]
- [ ]
- [ ]
- [ ]
- [ ]
- [ ]
- [ ]

SUNDAY, OCTOBER 1

MONDAY, OCTOBER 2

TUESDAY, OCTOBER 3

WEDNESDAY, OCTOBER 4

THURSDAY, OCTOBER 5

FRIDAY, OCTOBER 6

SATURDAY, OCTOBER 7

to-do list

- [ ]
- [ ]
- [ ]
- [ ]
- [ ]
- [ ]
- [ ]
- [ ]
- [ ]
- [ ]
- [ ]
- [ ]
- [ ]
- [ ]
- [ ]
- [ ]
- [ ]

Each of you is now a new person. You are becoming more and more like your Creator, and you will understand him better.

COLOSSIANS 3:10 CEV

OCTOBER
2023

S	M	T	W	T	F	S
1	2	3	4	5	6	7
8	9	10	11	12	13	14
15	16	17	18	19	20	21
22	23	24	25	26	27	28
29	30	31				

Emotions rise and fall. Circumstances ebb and flow. But God is committed to you. His love and faithfulness never fail. By holding tightly to your faith, you can weather any storm.

to-do list

- [ ]
- [ ]
- [ ]
- [ ]
- [ ]
- [ ]
- [ ]
- [ ]
- [ ]
- [ ]
- [ ]
- [ ]
- [ ]
- [ ]
- [ ]
- [ ]
- [ ]

SUNDAY, OCTOBER 8

MONDAY, OCTOBER 9 *Columbus Day*

TUESDAY, OCTOBER 10

WEDNESDAY, OCTOBER 11

THURSDAY, OCTOBER 12

FRIDAY, OCTOBER 13

SATURDAY, OCTOBER 14

to-do list

- [ ]
- [ ]
- [ ]
- [ ]
- [ ]
- [ ]
- [ ]
- [ ]
- [ ]
- [ ]
- [ ]
- [ ]
- [ ]
- [ ]
- [ ]
- [ ]
- [ ]
- [ ]

*Cling to your faith
in Christ.*
1 TIMOTHY 1:19 NLT

OCTOBER
2023

S	M	T	W	T	F	S
1	2	3	4	5	6	7
8	9	10	11	12	13	14
15	16	17	18	19	20	21
22	23	24	25	26	27	28
29	30	31				

God's compassion runs even deeper than a mother's love. His loving care is passionate, powerful, and permanent for those who put their faith in Him.

to-do list

- ☐
- ☐
- ☐
- ☐
- ☐
- ☐
- ☐
- ☐
- ☐
- ☐
- ☐
- ☐
- ☐
- ☐
- ☐
- ☐
- ☐

SUNDAY, OCTOBER 15

MONDAY, OCTOBER 16

TUESDAY, OCTOBER 17

WEDNESDAY, OCTOBER 18

THURSDAY, OCTOBER 19

FRIDAY, OCTOBER 20

SATURDAY, OCTOBER 21

to-do list

☐
☐
☐
☐
☐
☐
☐
☐
☐
☐
☐
☐
☐
☐

"Can a mother forget the baby at her breast and have no compassion on the child she has borne? Though she may forget, I will not forget you!"

ISAIAH 49:15 NIV

OCTOBER
2023

S	M	T	W	T	F	S
1	2	3	4	5	6	7
8	9	10	11	12	13	14
15	16	17	18	19	20	21
22	23	24	25	26	27	28
29	30	31				

The depth of God's love for us rivals the enormity of His might. Regardless of the troubles that may surround you, you can be confident that God remains in charge, in control, and deeply in love.

to-do list

- ☐
- ☐
- ☐
- ☐
- ☐
- ☐
- ☐
- ☐
- ☐
- ☐
- ☐
- ☐
- ☐
- ☐
- ☐
- ☐
- ☐
- ☐
- ☐
- ☐

SUNDAY, OCTOBER 22

MONDAY, OCTOBER 23

TUESDAY, OCTOBER 24

WEDNESDAY, OCTOBER 25

THURSDAY, OCTOBER 26

FRIDAY, OCTOBER 27

SATURDAY, OCTOBER 28

- [ ]
- [ ]
- [ ]
- [ ]
- [ ]
- [ ]
- [ ]
- [ ]
- [ ]
- [ ]
- [ ]
- [ ]
- [ ]
- [ ]
- [ ]
- [ ]

The Fear-of-God builds up confidence, and makes a world safe for your children.

PROVERBS 14:26 MSG

NOVEMBER 2023

SUNDAY	MONDAY	TUESDAY	WEDNESDAY
29	30	31	1
5 _Daylight Saving Time Ends_	6	7 _Election Day_	8
12	13	14	15
19	20	21	22
26	27	28	29

notes

THURSDAY	FRIDAY	SATURDAY
2	3	4
9	10	11 *Veterans Day*
16	17	18
23	24	25
Thanksgiving Day 30	1	2

....

....

....

....

....

....

....

....

....

....

....

....

....

....

OCTOBER

S	M	T	W	T	F	S
1	2	3	4	5	6	7
8	9	10	11	12	13	14
15	16	17	18	19	20	21
22	23	24	25	26	27	28
29	30	31				

DECEMBER

S	M	T	W	T	F	S
					1	2
3	4	5	6	7	8	9
10	11	12	13	14	15	16
17	18	19	20	21	22	23
24	25	26	27	28	29	30
31						

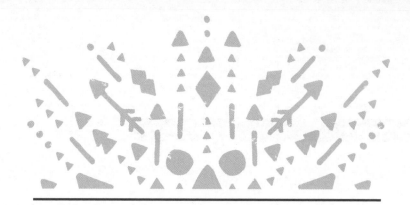

Limitless

There's only so much one woman can do. There are limits to your strength, your time, and your capacity to love others well. When you reach the limit of your own abilities, a feeling of helplessness can set in. But being helpless isn't synonymous with being hopeless. God is near. He hears every prayer, every longing, and every sigh. His power, love, and time are limitless. Cry out in faith when you need the comfort of your Father's love.

Goals *for the* Month

....

....

....

....

....

....

....

....

....

....

....

....

....

LORD, you know the hopes of the helpless. Surely
you will hear their cries and comfort them.
PSALM 10:17 NLT

NOVEMBER
2023

S	M	T	W	T	F	S
			1	2	3	4
5	6	7	8	9	10	11
12	13	14	15	16	17	18
19	20	21	22	23	24	25
26	27	28	29	30		

God's gifts are better than anything this world has to offer—filling your heart, instead of just your home.

to-do list

- [ ] ....
- [ ] ....
- [ ] ....
- [ ] ....
- [ ] ....
- [ ] ....
- [ ] ....
- [ ] ....
- [ ] ....
- [ ] ....
- [ ] ....
- [ ] ....
- [ ] ....
- [ ] ....
- [ ] ....
- [ ] ....
- [ ] ....
- [ ] ....

SUNDAY, OCTOBER 29

MONDAY, OCTOBER 30

TUESDAY, OCTOBER 31 *Halloween*

WEDNESDAY, NOVEMBER 1

....

....

....

....

....

THURSDAY, NOVEMBER 2

....

....

....

....

....

FRIDAY, NOVEMBER 3

....

....

....

....

....

SATURDAY, NOVEMBER 4

....

....

....

....

....

to-do list

☐
☐
☐
☐
☐
☐
☐
☐
☐
☐
☐
☐
☐
☐
☐
☐

*Godliness with
contentment is
great gain.*

1 TIMOTHY 6:6 NIV

NOVEMBER
2023

S	M	T	W	T	F	S
			1	2	3	4
5	6	7	8	9	10	11
12	13	14	15	16	17	18
19	20	21	22	23	24	25
26	27	28	29	30		

Through Christ, we can gather the courage to look at ourselves as we really are, faults and all, without shame. Being wholly loved gives us the courage to fully live.

to-do list

- [ ]
- [ ]
- [ ]
- [ ]
- [ ]
- [ ]
- [ ]
- [ ]
- [ ]
- [ ]
- [ ]
- [ ]
- [ ]
- [ ]
- [ ]
- [ ]
- [ ]
- [ ]

SUNDAY, NOVEMBER 5 *Daylight Saving Time Ends*

MONDAY, NOVEMBER 6

TUESDAY, NOVEMBER 7 *Election Day*

WEDNESDAY, NOVEMBER 8

....
....
....
....
....

THURSDAY, NOVEMBER 9

....
....
....
....
....

FRIDAY, NOVEMBER 10

....
....
....
....
....

SATURDAY, NOVEMBER 11 *Veterans Day*

....
....
....
....
....

to-do list

- [ ] ....
- [ ] ....
- [ ] ....
- [ ] ....
- [ ] ....
- [ ] ....
- [ ] ....
- [ ] ....
- [ ] ....
- [ ] ....
- [ ] ....
- [ ] ....
- [ ] ....
- [ ] ....

The blood of Jesus gives us courage to enter the most holy place by a new way that leads to life! And this way takes us through the curtain that is Christ himself.

HEBREWS 10:19–20 CEV

NOVEMBER
2023

S	M	T	W	T	F	S
			1	2	3	4
5	6	7	8	9	10	11
12	13	14	15	16	17	18
19	20	21	22	23	24	25
26	27	28	29	30		

When you're tempted to turn away from your problems, let faith help you turn toward God. With Him, you'll find the courage you need to do whatever needs to be done.

to-do list

- [ ]
- [ ]
- [ ]
- [ ]
- [ ]
- [ ]
- [ ]
- [ ]
- [ ]
- [ ]
- [ ]
- [ ]
- [ ]
- [ ]
- [ ]
- [ ]
- [ ]
- [ ]

SUNDAY, NOVEMBER 12

MONDAY, NOVEMBER 13

TUESDAY, NOVEMBER 14

WEDNESDAY, NOVEMBER 15

THURSDAY, NOVEMBER 16

FRIDAY, NOVEMBER 17

SATURDAY, NOVEMBER 18

to-do list

☐
☐
☐
☐
☐
☐
☐
☐
☐
☐
☐
☐
☐
☐
☐
☐

When I asked for your help, you answered my prayer and gave me courage.

PSALM 138:3 CEV

NOVEMBER
2023

S	M	T	W	T	F	S
			1	2	3	4
5	6	7	8	9	10	11
12	13	14	15	16	17	18
19	20	21	22	23	24	25
26	27	28	29	30		

God's only given you one life. Instead of living for "someday," God challenges you to put your heart into today.

to-do list

- ☐
- ☐
- ☐
- ☐
- ☐
- ☐
- ☐
- ☐
- ☐
- ☐
- ☐
- ☐
- ☐
- ☐
- ☐
- ☐
- ☐

SUNDAY, NOVEMBER 19

MONDAY, NOVEMBER 20

TUESDAY, NOVEMBER 21

WEDNESDAY, NOVEMBER 22

....
....
....
....
....

THURSDAY, NOVEMBER 23   *Thanksgiving Day*

....
....
....
....
....

FRIDAY, NOVEMBER 24

....
....
....
....
....

SATURDAY, NOVEMBER 25

....
....
....
....
....

to-do list

☐
☐
☐
☐
☐
☐
☐
☐
☐
☐
☐
☐
☐
☐
☐
☐

*Better is one day in
your courts than a
thousand elsewhere.*

PSALM 84:10 NIV

NOVEMBER

2023

S	M	T	W	T	F	S
			1	2	3	4
5	6	7	8	9	10	11
12	13	14	15	16	17	18
19	20	21	22	23	24	25
26	27	28	29	30		

Rest in the knowledge that God is working behind the scenes to bring about good in your life. The best decision you'll ever make is to trust in His love for you.

to-do list

- [ ] ....
- [ ] ....
- [ ] ....
- [ ] ....
- [ ] ....
- [ ] ....
- [ ] ....
- [ ] ....
- [ ] ....
- [ ] ....
- [ ] ....
- [ ] ....
- [ ] ....
- [ ] ....
- [ ] ....
- [ ] ....
- [ ] ....

SUNDAY, NOVEMBER 26

MONDAY, NOVEMBER 27

TUESDAY, NOVEMBER 28

WEDNESDAY, NOVEMBER 29

THURSDAY, NOVEMBER 30

FRIDAY, DECEMBER 1

SATURDAY, DECEMBER 2

to-do list

☐
☐
☐
☐
☐
☐
☐
☐
☐
☐
☐
☐
☐
☐
☐
☐

We make our own decisions, but the LORD alone determines what happens.

PROVERBS 16:33 CEV

DECEMBER 2023

SUNDAY	MONDAY	TUESDAY	WEDNESDAY
26	27	28	29
3	4	5	6
10	11	12	13
17	18	19	20
24 *Christmas Eve* / 31 *New Year's Eve*	25 *Christmas Day*	26	27

THURSDAY	FRIDAY	SATURDAY
30	1	2
7 *Hanukkah Begins at Sundown*	8	9
14	15	16
21 *First Day of Winter*	22	23
28	29	30

NOVEMBER

S	M	T	W	T	F	S
			1	2	3	4
5	6	7	8	9	10	11
12	13	14	15	16	17	18
19	20	21	22	23	24	25
26	27	28	29	30		

JANUARY

S	M	T	W	T	F	S
	1	2	3	4	5	6
7	8	9	10	11	12	13
14	15	16	17	18	19	20
21	22	23	24	25	26	27
28	29	30	31			

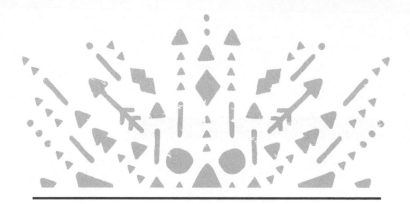

Follow Through

In the Bible, God asks people to do some pretty unlikely things. Build an ark. Defeat Jericho by walking around its walls. Battle a giant with a slingshot. But when people are committed to doing what God asks, amazing things happen. What's God asking you to do? Love someone who seems unlovable? Break a bad habit? Forgive? Commit yourself to follow through and do what God asks. Through faith, you'll witness firsthand how the unbelievable can happen.

Goals *for the* Month

....
....
....
....
....
....
....
....
....
....
....
....

*By faith the walls of Jericho fell, after the army
had marched around them for seven days.*

HEBREWS 11:30 NIV

DECEMBER
2023

S	M	T	W	T	F	S
					1	2
3	4	5	6	7	8	9
10	11	12	13	14	15	16
17	18	19	20	21	22	23
24	25	26	27	28	29	30
31						

The more you allow your faith to influence the decisions you make, the closer you'll be to living the life God desires for you. Invite God into your decision process.

to-do list

- [ ]
- [ ]
- [ ]
- [ ]
- [ ]
- [ ]
- [ ]
- [ ]
- [ ]
- [ ]
- [ ]
- [ ]
- [ ]
- [ ]
- [ ]
- [ ]
- [ ]

SUNDAY, DECEMBER 3

MONDAY, DECEMBER 4

TUESDAY, DECEMBER 5

WEDNESDAY, DECEMBER 6

THURSDAY, DECEMBER 7 *Hanukkah Begins at Sundown*

FRIDAY, DECEMBER 8

SATURDAY, DECEMBER 9

to-do list

I pray that your love will keep on growing and you will fully know and understand how to make the right choices.

PHILIPPIANS 1:9–10 CEV

DECEMBER
2023

S	M	T	W	T	F	S
					1	2
3	4	5	6	7	8	9
10	11	12	13	14	15	16
17	18	19	20	21	22	23
24	25	26	27	28	29	30
31						

God is the only one whose love for you will never waver. You're His treasure and His desire is to spend eternity with you.

to-do list

- ☐
- ☐
- ☐
- ☐
- ☐
- ☐
- ☐
- ☐
- ☐
- ☐
- ☐
- ☐
- ☐
- ☐
- ☐
- ☐
- ☐

SUNDAY, DECEMBER 10

MONDAY, DECEMBER 11

TUESDAY, DECEMBER 12

WEDNESDAY, DECEMBER 13

....

....

....

....

....

THURSDAY, DECEMBER 14

....

....

....

....

....

FRIDAY, DECEMBER 15

....

....

....

....

....

SATURDAY, DECEMBER 16

....

....

....

....

....

to-do list

- [ ] ....
- [ ] ....
- [ ] ....
- [ ] ....
- [ ] ....
- [ ] ....
- [ ] ....
- [ ] ....
- [ ] ....
- [ ] ....
- [ ] ....
- [ ] ....
- [ ] ....
- [ ] ....
- [ ] ....
- [ ] ....

"Wherever your treasure is, there the desires of your heart will also be."

MATTHEW 6:21 NLT

DECEMBER
2023

S	M	T	W	T	F	S
					1	2
3	4	5	6	7	8	9
10	11	12	13	14	15	16
17	18	19	20	21	22	23
24	25	26	27	28	29	30
31						

As you allow God to work in and through you, your desires begin to fall in line with His own. You're free to be exactly who God created you to be.

to-do list

- ☐
- ☐
- ☐
- ☐
- ☐
- ☐
- ☐
- ☐
- ☐
- ☐
- ☐
- ☐
- ☐
- ☐
- ☐
- ☐
- ☐
- ☐

SUNDAY, DECEMBER 17

MONDAY, DECEMBER 18

TUESDAY, DECEMBER 19

WEDNESDAY, DECEMBER 20

....
....
....
....
....

THURSDAY, DECEMBER 21   *First Day of Winter*

....
....
....
....
....

FRIDAY, DECEMBER 22

....
....
....
....
....

SATURDAY, DECEMBER 23

....
....
....
....
....

to-do list

- [ ]
- [ ]
- [ ]
- [ ]
- [ ]
- [ ]
- [ ]
- [ ]
- [ ]
- [ ]
- [ ]
- [ ]
- [ ]
- [ ]
- [ ]
- [ ]
- [ ]

You are no longer ruled by your desires, but by God's Spirit, who lives in you.

ROMANS 8:9 CEV

DECEMBER
2023

S	M	T	W	T	F	S
					1	2
3	4	5	6	7	8	9
10	11	12	13	14	15	16
17	18	19	20	21	22	23
24	25	26	27	28	29	30
31						

Your spiritual faith is a commitment
to love God. And since the word
love is a verb, an action word, your
devotion to God is faith on the move.
Where will faith move you today?

to-do list

- [ ]
- [ ]
- [ ]
- [ ]
- [ ]
- [ ]
- [ ]
- [ ]
- [ ]
- [ ]
- [ ]
- [ ]
- [ ]
- [ ]
- [ ]
- [ ]
- [ ]
- [ ]

SUNDAY, DECEMBER 24   *Christmas Eve*

MONDAY, DECEMBER 25   *Christmas Day*

TUESDAY, DECEMBER 26

WEDNESDAY, DECEMBER 27

THURSDAY, DECEMBER 28

FRIDAY, DECEMBER 29

SATURDAY, DECEMBER 30

to-do list

All the believers devoted themselves to the apostles' teaching, and to fellowship, and to sharing in meals . . .and to prayer.

ACTS 2:42 NLT

JANUARY 2024

SUNDAY	MONDAY	TUESDAY	WEDNESDAY
31	1 *New Year's Day*	2	3
7	8	9	10
14	15 *Martin Luther King Jr. Day*	16	17
21	22	23	24
28	29	30	31

notes

THURSDAY	FRIDAY	SATURDAY
4	5	6
11	12	13
18	19	20
25	26	27
1	2	3

....
....
....
....
....
....
....
....
....
....
....
....
....
....
....

DECEMBER

S	M	T	W	T	F	S
					1	2
3	4	5	6	7	8	9
10	11	12	13	14	15	16
17	18	19	20	21	22	23
24	25	26	27	28	29	30
31						

FEBRUARY

S	M	T	W	T	F	S
				1	2	3
4	5	6	7	8	9	10
11	12	13	14	15	16	17
18	19	20	21	22	23	24
25	26	27	28	29		

Celebrate!

When you work hard toward completing a goal, accomplishing what you've set out to do is something worth celebrating. When your accomplishment is fueled by faith, you can be certain you'll never celebrate alone. God sees the time, energy, and heart you put into your work. Better yet, He adds His own power to your efforts. This means that with God, you can accomplish things you could never do solely on your own. That's something truly worth celebrating—*with God!*

Goals *for the* Month

....
....
....
....
....
....
....
....
....
....
....
....
....
....

*We remember before our God and Father
your work produced by faith, your labor
prompted by love, and your endurance
inspired by hope in our Lord Jesus Christ.*
1 Thessalonians 1:3 niv

JANUARY
2024

S	M	T	W	T	F	S
	1	2	3	4	5	6
7	8	9	10	11	12	13
14	15	16	17	18	19	20
21	22	23	24	25	26	27
28	29	30	31			

Bring every doubt and worry to God in prayer. Allow Him to transform your doubts into faith.

to-do list

- [ ]
- [ ]
- [ ]
- [ ]
- [ ]
- [ ]
- [ ]
- [ ]
- [ ]
- [ ]
- [ ]
- [ ]
- [ ]
- [ ]
- [ ]
- [ ]
- [ ]
- [ ]
- [ ]

SUNDAY, DECEMBER 31   *New Year's Eve*

MONDAY, JANUARY 1   *New Year's Day*

TUESDAY, JANUARY 2

WEDNESDAY, JANUARY 3'

THURSDAY, JANUARY 4

FRIDAY, JANUARY 5

SATURDAY, JANUARY 6

to-do list

☐
☐
☐
☐
☐
☐
☐
☐
☐
☐
☐
☐
☐
☐
☐
☐

*Immediately the father
of the child cried out
and said with tears,
"Lord, I believe; help
my unbelief!"*

MARK 9:24 NKJV

JANUARY

2024

S	M	T	W	T	F	S
	1	2	3	4	5	6
7	8	9	10	11	12	13
14	15	16	17	18	19	20
21	22	23	24	25	26	27
28	29	30	31			

God cares for you because He cares
about you. Let that fact encourage
you in your faith today.

to-do list

- .... ☐
- .... ☐
- .... ☐
- .... ☐
- .... ☐
- .... ☐
- .... ☐
- .... ☐
- .... ☐
- .... ☐
- .... ☐
- .... ☐
- .... ☐
- .... ☐
- .... ☐
- .... ☐
- .... ☐
- .... ☐
- .... ☐

SUNDAY, JANUARY 7

MONDAY, JANUARY 8

TUESDAY, JANUARY 9

WEDNESDAY, JANUARY 10

THURSDAY, JANUARY 11

FRIDAY, JANUARY 12

SATURDAY, JANUARY 13

to-do list

- [ ]
- [ ]
- [ ]
- [ ]
- [ ]
- [ ]
- [ ]
- [ ]
- [ ]
- [ ]
- [ ]
- [ ]
- [ ]
- [ ]
- [ ]

The humble will see their God at work and be glad. Let all who seek God's help be encouraged.

PSALM 69:32 NLT

JANUARY

2024

S	M	T	W	T	F	S
	1	2	3	4	5	6
7	8	9	10	11	12	13
14	15	16	17	18	19	20
21	22	23	24	25	26	27
28	29	30	31			

Once your faith sets you on the path toward heaven, nothing—absolutely *nothing*—can prevent you from reaching your destination.

to-do list

☐
☐
☐
☐
☐
☐
☐
☐
☐
☐
☐
☐
☐
☐
☐
☐
☐
☐

SUNDAY, JANUARY 14

MONDAY, JANUARY 15   *Martin Luther King Jr. Day*

TUESDAY, JANUARY 16

WEDNESDAY, JANUARY 17

....
....
....
....
....

THURSDAY, JANUARY 18

....
....
....
....
....

FRIDAY, JANUARY 19

....
....
....
....
....

SATURDAY, JANUARY 20

....
....
....
....
....

to-do list

- [ ] ....
- [ ] ....
- [ ] ....
- [ ] ....
- [ ] ....
- [ ] ....
- [ ] ....
- [ ] ....
- [ ] ....
- [ ] ....
- [ ] ....
- [ ] ....
- [ ] ....
- [ ] ....

God loved the people of this world so much that he gave his only Son, so that everyone who has faith in him will have eternal life and never really die.

JOHN 3:16 CEV

JANUARY
2024

S	M	T	W	T	F	S
	1	2	3	4	5	6
7	8	9	10	11	12	13
14	15	16	17	18	19	20
21	22	23	24	25	26	27
28	29	30	31			

Jesus never treats people like an
interruption or inconvenience.
He listens, comforts, and cares.

to-do list

- .... ☐
- .... ☐
- .... ☐
- .... ☐
- .... ☐
- .... ☐
- .... ☐
- .... ☐
- .... ☐
- .... ☐
- .... ☐
- .... ☐
- .... ☐
- .... ☐
- .... ☐
- .... ☐
- .... ☐
- .... ☐

SUNDAY, JANUARY 21

MONDAY, JANUARY 22

TUESDAY, JANUARY 23

WEDNESDAY, JANUARY 24

....
....
....
....
....

THURSDAY, JANUARY 25

....
....
....
....
....

FRIDAY, JANUARY 26

....
....
....
....
....

SATURDAY, JANUARY 27

....
....
....
....
....

to-do list

- [ ]
- [ ]
- [ ]
- [ ]
- [ ]
- [ ]
- [ ]
- [ ]
- [ ]
- [ ]
- [ ]
- [ ]
- [ ]
- [ ]
- [ ]
- [ ]

*Follow the example of
the correct teaching I
gave you, and let the
faith and love of Christ
Jesus be your model.*

2 TIMOTHY 1:13 CEV

FEBRUARY 2024

SUNDAY	MONDAY	TUESDAY	WEDNESDAY
28	29	30	31
4	5	6	7
11	12	13	14 *Valentine's Day* *Ash Wednesday*
18	19 *Presidents' Day*	20	21
25	26	27	28

THURSDAY	FRIDAY	SATURDAY
1	2	3
8	9	10
15	16	17
22	23	24
29	1	2
Leap Day		

JANUARY

S	M	T	W	T	F	S
	1	2	3	4	5	6
7	8	9	10	11	12	13
14	15	16	17	18	19	20
21	22	23	24	25	26	27
28	29	30	31			

MARCH

S	M	T	W	T	F	S
					1	2
3	4	5	6	7	8	9
10	11	12	13	14	15	16
17	18	19	20	21	22	23
24	25	26	27	28	29	30
31						

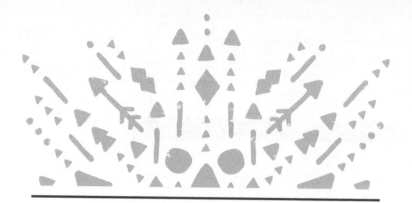

God-Confidence

You're a beautiful, gifted woman. God created you that way. You have countless reasons to be confident in what you do, who you are, and where you're headed—but those reasons don't rest on your talents, intelligence, accomplishments, net worth, or good looks. They rest solely on God and His faithfulness. Living a life of faith means trading self-confidence for God-confidence. It means holding your head high because you know you're loved and that God's Spirit is working through you.

Goals *for the* Month

....
....
....
....
....
....
....
....
....
....
....
....
....
....
....
....

Forget about self-confidence; it's useless.
Cultivate God-confidence.
1 CORINTHIANS 10:12 MSG

FEBRUARY

S	M	T	W	T	F	S
				1	2	3
4	5	6	7	8	9	10
11	12	13	14	15	16	17
18	19	20	21	22	23	24
25	26	27	28	29		

Keep your eyes open and your heart expectant. Don't miss out on the joy of catching a glimpse of God at work.

to-do list

- [ ] ....
- [ ] ....
- [ ] ....
- [ ] ....
- [ ] ....
- [ ] ....
- [ ] ....
- [ ] ....
- [ ] ....
- [ ] ....
- [ ] ....
- [ ] ....
- [ ] ....
- [ ] ....
- [ ] ....
- [ ] ....
- [ ] ....
- [ ] ....

SUNDAY, JANUARY 28

MONDAY, JANUARY 29

TUESDAY, JANUARY 30

WEDNESDAY, JANUARY 31

....
....
....
....
....

THURSDAY, FEBRUARY 1

....
....
....
....
....

FRIDAY, FEBRUARY 2

....
....
....
....
....

SATURDAY, FEBRUARY 3

....
....
....
....
....

to-do list

- ☐
- ☐
- ☐
- ☐
- ☐
- ☐
- ☐
- ☐
- ☐
- ☐
- ☐
- ☐
- ☐
- ☐
- ☐
- ☐
- ☐

*In the morning, LORD,
you hear my voice; in
the morning I lay my
requests before you
and wait expectantly.*

PSALM 5:3 NIV

FEBRUARY 2024

S	M	T	W	T	F	S
				1	2	3
4	5	6	7	8	9	10
11	12	13	14	15	16	17
18	19	20	21	22	23	24
25	26	27	28	29		

With God's help, you can become a woman others can depend on. Including God. Live out your faith by becoming more faithful.

to-do list

- [ ] ....
- [ ] ....
- [ ] ....
- [ ] ....
- [ ] ....
- [ ] ....
- [ ] ....
- [ ] ....
- [ ] ....
- [ ] ....
- [ ] ....
- [ ] ....
- [ ] ....
- [ ] ....
- [ ] ....
- [ ] ....
- [ ] ....
- [ ] ....

SUNDAY, FEBRUARY 4

MONDAY, FEBRUARY 5

TUESDAY, FEBRUARY 6

WEDNESDAY, FEBRUARY 7

....
....
....
....
....

THURSDAY, FEBRUARY 8

....
....
....
....
....

FRIDAY, FEBRUARY 9

....
....
....
....
....

SATURDAY, FEBRUARY 10

....
....
....
....
....

to-do list

☐
☐
☐
☐
☐
☐
☐
☐
☐
☐
☐
☐
☐
☐
☐
☐

Let love and faithfulness never leave you; bind them around your neck, write them on the tablet of your heart.

PROVERBS 3:3 NIV

FEBRUARY

S	M	T	W	T	F	S
				1	2	3
4	5	6	7	8	9	10
11	12	13	14	15	16	17
18	19	20	21	22	23	24
25	26	27	28	29		

It takes God's wisdom to balance the power of your emotions. When emotions run high, ask God for control and clarity before you act.

to-do list

- ☐ ....
- ☐ ....
- ☐ ....
- ☐ ....
- ☐ ....
- ☐ ....
- ☐ ....
- ☐ ....
- ☐ ....
- ☐ ....
- ☐ ....
- ☐ ....
- ☐ ....
- ☐ ....
- ☐ ....
- ☐ ....
- ☐ ....
- ☐ ....
- ☐ ....

SUNDAY, FEBRUARY 11

MONDAY, FEBRUARY 12

TUESDAY, FEBRUARY 13

WEDNESDAY, FEBRUARY 14

Valentine's Day
Ash Wednesday

....

....

....

....

....

THURSDAY, FEBRUARY 15

....

....

....

....

....

FRIDAY, FEBRUARY 16

....

....

....

....

....

SATURDAY, FEBRUARY 17

....

....

....

....

....

to-do list

- ☐ ....
- ☐ ....
- ☐ ....
- ☐ ....
- ☐ ....
- ☐ ....
- ☐ ....
- ☐ ....
- ☐ ....
- ☐ ....
- ☐ ....
- ☐ ....
- ☐ ....
- ☐ ....
- ☐ ....
- ☐ ....

But even if we don't feel at ease, God is greater than our feelings, and he knows everything.

1 JOHN 3:20 CEV

FEBRUARY
2024

S	M	T	W	T	F	S
				1	2	3
4	5	6	7	8	9	10
11	12	13	14	15	16	17
18	19	20	21	22	23	24
25	26	27	28	29		

Being generous in sharing our time, our resources, and our experiences helps God's family grow stronger as a whole. As we hold on loosely to what we've been given, our arms will be more able to hold on tightly to those around us.

to-do list

- [ ]
- [ ]
- [ ]
- [ ]
- [ ]
- [ ]
- [ ]
- [ ]
- [ ]
- [ ]
- [ ]
- [ ]
- [ ]
- [ ]
- [ ]
- [ ]
- [ ]
- [ ]
- [ ]

SUNDAY, FEBRUARY 18

MONDAY, FEBRUARY 19   *Presidents' Day*

TUESDAY, FEBRUARY 20

WEDNESDAY, FEBRUARY 21

THURSDAY, FEBRUARY 22

FRIDAY, FEBRUARY 23

SATURDAY, FEBRUARY 24

to-do list

☐
☐
☐
☐
☐
☐
☐
☐
☐
☐
☐
☐
☐
☐
☐
☐

All the Lord's followers
often met together,
and they shared
everything they had.
ACTS 2:44 CEV

FEBRUARY
2024

S	M	T	W	T	F	S
				1	2	3
4	5	6	7	8	9	10
11	12	13	14	15	16	17
18	19	20	21	22	23	24
25	26	27	28	29		

When we focus on our wants, we become a slave to those longings. There's only "one thing" that truly satisfies—having faith in the God who loves you enough to provide exactly what you need.

to-do list

- [ ]
- [ ]
- [ ]
- [ ]
- [ ]
- [ ]
- [ ]
- [ ]
- [ ]
- [ ]
- [ ]
- [ ]
- [ ]
- [ ]
- [ ]
- [ ]
- [ ]
- [ ]

SUNDAY, FEBRUARY 25

MONDAY, FEBRUARY 26

TUESDAY, FEBRUARY 27

WEDNESDAY, FEBRUARY 28

THURSDAY, FEBRUARY 29   *Leap Day*

FRIDAY, MARCH 1

SATURDAY, MARCH 2

to-do list

- [ ]
- [ ]
- [ ]
- [ ]
- [ ]
- [ ]
- [ ]
- [ ]
- [ ]
- [ ]
- [ ]
- [ ]
- [ ]
- [ ]
- [ ]
- [ ]

"No one can serve two masters. . . . You cannot serve both God and money."

MATTHEW 6:24 NIV

MARCH 2024

SUNDAY	MONDAY	TUESDAY	WEDNESDAY
25	26	27	28
3	4	5	6
10 *Daylight Saving Time Begins*	11	12	13
17 *St. Patrick's Day*	18	19 *First Day of Spring*	20
24 *Palm Sunday* / *Easter Sunday* 31	25	26	27

notes

THURSDAY	FRIDAY	SATURDAY
29	1	2
7	8	9
14	15	16
21	22	23
28	29	30
	Good Friday	

....
....
....
....
....
....
....
....
....
....
....
....
....
....
....
....
....

FEBRUARY

S	M	T	W	T	F	S
				1	2	3
4	5	6	7	8	9	10
11	12	13	14	15	16	17
18	19	20	21	22	23	24
25	26	27	28	29		

APRIL

S	M	T	W	T	F	S
	1	2	3	4	5	6
7	8	9	10	11	12	13
14	15	16	17	18	19	20
21	22	23	24	25	26	27
28	29	30				

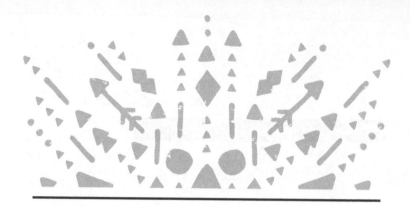

Into His Arms

Every walk you take is a series of steps that moves you forward. Each day you live is like a single step, moving you closer to—or farther away—from God. That's why it's good to get your bearings each morning. Through reading the Bible and spending time with God in prayer, you'll know which direction to take as you continue your walk of faith. Day by day, God will guide you straight into His arms.

Goals *for the* Month

....
....
....
....
....
....
....
....
....
....
....
....
....
....
....
....

"Love the LORD your God, walk in all his ways,
obey his commands, hold firmly to him, and serve
him with all your heart and all your soul."

JOSHUA 22:5 NLT

MARCH
2024

S	M	T	W	T	F	S
					1	2
3	4	5	6	7	8	9
10	11	12	13	14	15	16
17	18	19	20	21	22	23
24	25	26	27	28	29	30
31						

Faith can break a cycle of regrettable yesterdays—if we let it. God offers forgiveness and a fresh start to all who ask. He never tires of us bringing our brokenness to Him.

to-do list

- [ ] ....
- [ ] ....
- [ ] ....
- [ ] ....
- [ ] ....
- [ ] ....
- [ ] ....
- [ ] ....
- [ ] ....
- [ ] ....
- [ ] ....
- [ ] ....
- [ ] ....
- [ ] ....
- [ ] ....
- [ ] ....
- [ ] ....
- [ ] ....

SUNDAY, MARCH 3

MONDAY, MARCH 4

TUESDAY, MARCH 5

WEDNESDAY, MARCH 6

....
....
....
....
....

THURSDAY, MARCH 7

....
....
....
....
....

FRIDAY, MARCH 8

....
....
....
....
....

SATURDAY, MARCH 9

....
....
....
....
....

to-do list

- ☐
- ☐
- ☐
- ☐
- ☐
- ☐
- ☐
- ☐
- ☐
- ☐
- ☐
- ☐
- ☐

The faithful love of the LORD never ends! His mercies never cease. Great is his faithfulness; his mercies begin afresh each morning.

LAMENTATIONS 3:22–23 NLT

MARCH 2024

S	M	T	W	T	F	S
					1	2
3	4	5	6	7	8	9
10	11	12	13	14	15	16
17	18	19	20	21	22	23
24	25	26	27	28	29	30
31						

Follow Jesus' example. . .and no matter how busy you get, make time for the friends God brings into your life. They may be God's answers to prayers you're praying today.

to-do list

- [ ] ....
- [ ] ....
- [ ] ....
- [ ] ....
- [ ] ....
- [ ] ....
- [ ] ....
- [ ] ....
- [ ] ....
- [ ] ....
- [ ] ....
- [ ] ....
- [ ] ....
- [ ] ....
- [ ] ....
- [ ] ....
- [ ] ....
- [ ] ....

SUNDAY, MARCH 10 *Daylight Saving Time Begins*

MONDAY, MARCH 11

TUESDAY, MARCH 12

WEDNESDAY, MARCH 13

THURSDAY, MARCH 14

FRIDAY, MARCH 15

SATURDAY, MARCH 16

to-do list

- [ ]
- [ ]
- [ ]
- [ ]
- [ ]
- [ ]
- [ ]
- [ ]
- [ ]
- [ ]
- [ ]
- [ ]
- [ ]
- [ ]
- [ ]
- [ ]

Just as lotions and fragrance give sensual delight, a sweet friendship refreshes the soul.

PROVERBS 27:9 MSG

MARCH
2024

S	M	T	W	T	F	S
					1	2
3	4	5	6	7	8	9
10	11	12	13	14	15	16
17	18	19	20	21	22	23
24	25	26	27	28	29	30
31						

God holds our future in His hands. He has a plan and a purpose for what lies ahead. We may not know the details of all our tomorrows, but faith assures us it's well worth waiting for.

to-do list

☐
☐
☐
☐
☐
☐
☐
☐
☐
☐
☐
☐
☐
☐
☐
☐
☐
☐

SUNDAY, MARCH 17 *St. Patrick's Day*

MONDAY, MARCH 18

TUESDAY, MARCH 19 *First Day of Spring*

WEDNESDAY, MARCH 20

THURSDAY, MARCH 21

FRIDAY, MARCH 22

SATURDAY, MARCH 23

to-do list

- [ ]
- [ ]
- [ ]
- [ ]
- [ ]
- [ ]
- [ ]
- [ ]
- [ ]
- [ ]
- [ ]
- [ ]
- [ ]
- [ ]

"For I know the plans I have for you," declares the Lord, "plans to prosper you and not to harm you, plans to give you hope and a future."

JEREMIAH 29:11 NIV

MARCH
2024

S	M	T	W	T	F	S
					1	2
3	4	5	6	7	8	9
10	11	12	13	14	15	16
17	18	19	20	21	22	23
24	25	26	27	28	29	30
31						

Whether it's your time, your finances, your home—or things like forgiveness, grace, or love—follow God's example. Be big hearted and open handed.

to-do list

- [ ] ....
- [ ] ....
- [ ] ....
- [ ] ....
- [ ] ....
- [ ] ....
- [ ] ....
- [ ] ....
- [ ] ....
- [ ] ....
- [ ] ....
- [ ] ....
- [ ] ....
- [ ] ....
- [ ] ....
- [ ] ....
- [ ] ....

SUNDAY, MARCH 24 *Palm Sunday*

MONDAY, MARCH 25

TUESDAY, MARCH 26

WEDNESDAY, MARCH 27

THURSDAY, MARCH 28

FRIDAY, MARCH 29   *Good Friday*

SATURDAY, MARCH 30

to-do list

- [ ]
- [ ]
- [ ]
- [ ]
- [ ]
- [ ]
- [ ]
- [ ]
- [ ]
- [ ]
- [ ]
- [ ]
- [ ]
- [ ]
- [ ]

I am praying that you will put into action the generosity that comes from your faith as you understand and experience all the good things we have in Christ.

PHILEMON 1:6 NLT

APRIL 2024

SUNDAY	MONDAY	TUESDAY	WEDNESDAY
31	1	2	3
7	8	9	10
14	15	16	17
21	22 *Passover Begins at Sundown*	23	24
28	29	30	1

notes

THURSDAY	FRIDAY	SATURDAY
4	5	6
11	12	13
18	19	20
25	26	27
2	3	4

....
....
....
....
....
....
....
....
....
....
....
....
....

MARCH

S	M	T	W	T	F	S
					1	2
3	4	5	6	7	8	9
10	11	12	13	14	15	16
17	18	19	20	21	22	23
24	25	26	27	28	29	30
31						

MAY

S	M	T	W	T	F	S
			1	2	3	4
5	6	7	8	9	10	11
12	13	14	15	16	17	18
19	20	21	22	23	24	25
26	27	28	29	30	31	

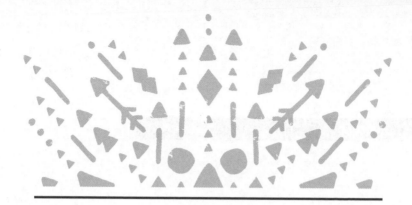

Devoted to Others

Our devotion to God leads us to be more devoted to others. That's because God's Spirit is at work in us, encouraging us to do what's right. When we keep our promises, weigh our words, and offer a helping hand with no expectation of reward, we are loving God by loving others. Our faith-filled devotion to God brings out the best in us, while at the same time blessing those around us.

Goals *for the* Month

....

....

....

....

....

....

....

....

....

....

....

....

....

....

....

Women who claim to be devoted to God should make themselves attractive by the good things they do.
1 TIMOTHY 2:10 NLT

APRIL *2024*

S	M	T	W	T	F	S
	1	2	3	4	5	6
7	8	9	10	11	12	13
14	15	16	17	18	19	20
21	22	23	24	25	26	27
28	29	30				

When you tell God, "I believe," His grace wipes away everything that once came between you and Him. Lies. Anger. Betrayal. Pride. Selfishness. They're history, by God's grace alone.

to-do list

- [ ] ....
- [ ] ....
- [ ] ....
- [ ] ....
- [ ] ....
- [ ] ....
- [ ] ....
- [ ] ....
- [ ] ....
- [ ] ....
- [ ] ....
- [ ] ....
- [ ] ....
- [ ] ....
- [ ] ....
- [ ] ....
- [ ] ....
- [ ] ....
- [ ] ....

SUNDAY, MARCH 31 *Easter Sunday*

MONDAY, APRIL 1

TUESDAY, APRIL 2

WEDNESDAY, APRIL 3

THURSDAY, APRIL 4

FRIDAY, APRIL 5

SATURDAY, APRIL 6

to-do list

☐
☐
☐
☐
☐
☐
☐
☐
☐
☐
☐
☐
☐
☐
☐
☐

*God saved you by
his grace when you
believed. And you can't
take credit for this;
it is a gift from God.*

EPHESIANS 2:8 NLT

APRIL *2024*

S	M	T	W	T	F	S
	1	2	3	4	5	6
7	8	9	10	11	12	13
14	15	16	17	18	19	20
21	22	23	24	25	26	27
28	29	30				

Though happiness is often dependent on circumstances, when your journey is guided by faith you can find yourself feeling happy at the most unexpected moments. Where will God surprise you with happiness today?

to-do list

- [ ] ....
- [ ] ....
- [ ] ....
- [ ] ....
- [ ] ....
- [ ] ....
- [ ] ....
- [ ] ....
- [ ] ....
- [ ] ....
- [ ] ....
- [ ] ....
- [ ] ....
- [ ] ....
- [ ] ....
- [ ] ....
- [ ] ....
- [ ] ....

SUNDAY, APRIL 7

MONDAY, APRIL 8

TUESDAY, APRIL 9

WEDNESDAY, APRIL 10

THURSDAY, APRIL 11

FRIDAY, APRIL 12

SATURDAY, APRIL 13

to-do list

☐
☐
☐
☐
☐
☐
☐
☐
☐
☐
☐
☐
☐
☐

You will come to know God even better. His glorious power will make you patient and strong enough to endure anything, and you will be truly happy.

COLOSSIANS 1:10–11 CEV

APRIL 2024

S	M	T	W	T	F	S
	1	2	3	4	5	6
7	8	9	10	11	12	13
14	15	16	17	18	19	20
21	22	23	24	25	26	27
28	29	30				

Regardless of your circumstance—
big or small—don't wait until you
come to the end of your rope to pray.
Call out to Him anytime, anywhere.

to-do list

☐
☐
☐
☐
☐
☐
☐
☐
☐
☐
☐
☐
☐
☐
☐
☐
☐
☐

SUNDAY, APRIL 14

MONDAY, APRIL 15

TUESDAY, APRIL 16

WEDNESDAY, APRIL 17

THURSDAY, APRIL 18

FRIDAY, APRIL 19

SATURDAY, APRIL 20

to-do list

- [ ]
- [ ]
- [ ]
- [ ]
- [ ]
- [ ]
- [ ]
- [ ]
- [ ]
- [ ]
- [ ]
- [ ]
- [ ]
- [ ]
- [ ]
- [ ]

Get up and pray for help all through the night. Pour out your feelings to the Lord, as you would pour water out of a jug.

LAMENTATIONS 2:19 CEV

APRIL

S	M	T	W	T	F	S
	1	2	3	4	5	6
7	8	9	10	11	12	13
14	15	16	17	18	19	20
21	22	23	24	25	26	27
28	29	30				

God's presence can be a place of rest and refuge. Find a quiet spot to just sit. Then invite God to join you. Allow Him to refresh you with His love.

to-do list

- ☐
- ☐
- ☐
- ☐
- ☐
- ☐
- ☐
- ☐
- ☐
- ☐
- ☐
- ☐
- ☐
- ☐
- ☐
- ☐
- ☐
- ☐

SUNDAY, APRIL 21

MONDAY, APRIL 22 *Passover Begins at Sundown*

TUESDAY, APRIL 23

WEDNESDAY, APRIL 24

....
....
....
....
....

THURSDAY, APRIL 25

....
....
....
....
....

FRIDAY, APRIL 26

....
....
....
....
....

SATURDAY, APRIL 27

....
....
....
....
....

to-do list

☐
☐
☐
☐
☐
☐
☐
☐
☐
☐
☐
☐
☐
☐
☐
☐

God is our refuge and strength, a very present help in trouble.
PSALM 46:1 NKJV

MAY 2024

SUNDAY	MONDAY	TUESDAY	WEDNESDAY
28	29	30	1
5	6	7	8
12 *Mother's Day*	13	14	15
19	20	21	22
26	27 *Memorial Day*	28	29

THURSDAY	FRIDAY	SATURDAY
2 *National Day of Prayer*	3	4
9	10	11
16	17	18
23	24	25
30	31	1

....
....
....
....
....
....
....
....
....
....
....
....
....
....

APRIL

S	M	T	W	T	F	S
	1	2	3	4	5	6
7	8	9	10	11	12	13
14	15	16	17	18	19	20
21	22	23	24	25	26	27
28	29	30				

JUNE

S	M	T	W	T	F	S
						1
2	3	4	5	6	7	8
9	10	11	12	13	14	15
16	17	18	19	20	21	22
23	24	25	26	27	28	29
30						

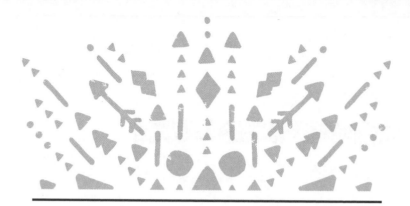

The Unexpected

What can we expect from God? The unexpected. Many people who came to Jesus asked to be healed. But how Jesus healed them was never the same. He put mud in a blind man's eyes. A bleeding woman merely touched His robe. Sometimes, Jesus spoke—and healing happened. Coming to God in faith means you can expect that He will act. He promises He'll respond to your prayers. How? Anticipate the unexpected.

Goals *for the* Month

....

....

....

....

....

....

....

....

....

....

....

....

....

Jesus replied, "Why do you say 'if you can'?
Anything is possible for someone who has faith!"
MARK 9:23 CEV

MAY 2024

S	M	T	W	T	F	S
			1	2	3	4
5	6	7	8	9	10	11
12	13	14	15	16	17	18
19	20	21	22	23	24	25
26	27	28	29	30	31	

God is the ultimate gardener. His focus is tending His children. Humbly allow Him to have His way in helping your faith grow.

to-do list

- ☐
- ☐
- ☐
- ☐
- ☐
- ☐
- ☐
- ☐
- ☐
- ☐
- ☐
- ☐
- ☐
- ☐
- ☐
- ☐
- ☐

SUNDAY, APRIL 28

MONDAY, APRIL 29

TUESDAY, APRIL 30

WEDNESDAY, MAY 1

....
....
....
....
....

THURSDAY, MAY 2   *National Day of Prayer*

....
....
....
....
....

FRIDAY, MAY 3

....
....
....
....
....

SATURDAY, MAY 4

....
....
....
....
....

to-do list

☐
☐
☐
☐
☐
☐
☐
☐
☐
☐
☐
☐
☐
☐
☐
☐

In simple humility, let our gardener, God, landscape you with the Word, making a salvation-garden of your life.

JAMES 1:21 MSG

MAY 2024

S	M	T	W	T	F	S
			1	2	3	4
5	6	7	8	9	10	11
12	13	14	15	16	17	18
19	20	21	22	23	24	25
26	27	28	29	30	31	

The more you depend on God, the deeper your well of joy. Ask God to show you how to draw on that reserve of joy, in any and every circumstance.

to-do list

- ☐
- ☐
- ☐
- ☐
- ☐
- ☐
- ☐
- ☐
- ☐
- ☐
- ☐
- ☐
- ☐
- ☐
- ☐
- ☐
- ☐
- ☐
- ☐

SUNDAY, MAY 5

MONDAY, MAY 6

TUESDAY, MAY 7

WEDNESDAY, MAY 8

THURSDAY, MAY 9

FRIDAY, MAY 10

SATURDAY, MAY 11

to-do list

- [ ]
- [ ]
- [ ]
- [ ]
- [ ]
- [ ]
- [ ]
- [ ]
- [ ]
- [ ]
- [ ]
- [ ]
- [ ]
- [ ]

Though you have not seen him, you love him; and even though you do not see him now, you believe in him and are filled with an inexpressible and glorious joy.

1 PETER 1:8 NIV

MAY

2024

S	M	T	W	T	F	S
			1	2	3	4
5	6	7	8	9	10	11
12	13	14	15	16	17	18
19	20	21	22	23	24	25
26	27	28	29	30	31	

God works in wonderfully unlikely ways. Regard troubles as opportunities, instead of obstacles. As you rely on God, His glory will shine through you—and unexpected joy will be your reward.

to-do list

- [ ] ....
- [ ] ....
- [ ] ....
- [ ] ....
- [ ] ....
- [ ] ....
- [ ] ....
- [ ] ....
- [ ] ....
- [ ] ....
- [ ] ....
- [ ] ....
- [ ] ....
- [ ] ....
- [ ] ....
- [ ] ....

SUNDAY, MAY 12 — *Mother's Day*

MONDAY, MAY 13

TUESDAY, MAY 14

WEDNESDAY, MAY 15

THURSDAY, MAY 16

FRIDAY, MAY 17

SATURDAY, MAY 18

to-do list

☐
☐
☐
☐
☐
☐
☐
☐
☐
☐
☐
☐
☐
☐

*When troubles. . .come
your way, consider
it an opportunity for
great joy. For you know
that when your faith is
tested, your endurance
has a chance to grow.*

JAMES 1:2–3 NLT

MAY 2024

S	M	T	W	T	F	S
			1	2	3	4
5	6	7	8	9	10	11
12	13	14	15	16	17	18
19	20	21	22	23	24	25
26	27	28	29	30	31	

If God places you in a position of leadership, whether at home, at work, at church, or in the community, recognize it for the privilege it is. Ask God to help you love those you lead, guiding them with humility and wisdom.

to-do list

- ☐
- ☐
- ☐
- ☐
- ☐
- ☐
- ☐
- ☐
- ☐
- ☐
- ☐
- ☐
- ☐
- ☐
- ☐
- ☐
- ☐

SUNDAY, MAY 19

MONDAY, MAY 20

TUESDAY, MAY 21

WEDNESDAY, MAY 22

THURSDAY, MAY 23

FRIDAY, MAY 24

SATURDAY, MAY 25

to-do list

- [ ]
- [ ]
- [ ]
- [ ]
- [ ]
- [ ]
- [ ]
- [ ]
- [ ]
- [ ]
- [ ]
- [ ]
- [ ]
- [ ]
- [ ]
- [ ]

If God has given you leadership ability, take the responsibility seriously.

ROMANS 12:8 NLT

MAY 2024

S	M	T	W	T	F	S
			· 1	2	3	4
5	6	7	8	9	10	11
12	13	14	15	16	17	18
19	20	21	22	23	24	25
26	27	28	29	30	31	

You may be lonely, but you're never alone. Find a place of solace in the silence through prayer. Loneliness may be the perfect lifeline to draw you closer to God, the one whose love will never fail.

to-do list

- ☐
- ☐
- ☐
- ☐
- ☐
- ☐
- ☐
- ☐
- ☐
- ☐
- ☐
- ☐
- ☐
- ☐
- ☐
- ☐
- ☐
- ☐

SUNDAY, MAY 26

MONDAY, MAY 27 *Memorial Day*

TUESDAY, MAY 28

WEDNESDAY, MAY 29

THURSDAY, MAY 30

FRIDAY, MAY 31

SATURDAY, JUNE 1

Jesus often withdrew to lonely places and prayed.
LUKE 5:16 NIV

JUNE 2024

SUNDAY	MONDAY	TUESDAY	WEDNESDAY
26	27	28	29
2	3	4	5
9	10	11	12
16	17	18	19
Father's Day 23	24	25	26
30			

notes

THURSDAY	FRIDAY	SATURDAY
30	31	1
6	7	8
13	14 Flag Day	15
20 First Day of Summer	21	22
27	28	29

....
....
....
....
....
....
....
....
....
....
....
....
....
....
....

MAY

S	M	T	W	T	F	S
			1	2	3	4
5	6	7	8	9	10	11
12	13	14	15	16	17	18
19	20	21	22	23	24	25
26	27	28	29	30	31	

JULY

S	M	T	W	T	F	S
	1	2	3	4	5	6
7	8	9	10	11	12	13
14	15	16	17	18	19	20
21	22	23	24	25	26	27
28	29	30	31			

Perfectly

God's faithfulness to you never falters. It began before you were born and will last far beyond the day you die. Nothing you do, or don't do, can adversely affect His love and devotion. This kind of faithfulness can only come from God. Those who love you may promise they'll never let you down, but they're fallible. Just like you. Only God is perfect—and perfectly trustworthy. What He says, He does. Today, tomorrow, always.

Goals *for the* Month

....

....

....

....

....

....

....

....

....

....

....

*Your kingdom is an everlasting kingdom,
and your dominion endures through all
generations. The LORD is trustworthy in all
he promises and faithful in all he does.*

PSALM 145:13 NIV

JUNE 2024

S	M	T	W	T	F	S
						1
2	3	4	5	6	7	8
9	10	11	12	13	14	15
16	17	18	19	20	21	22
23	24	25	26	27	28	29
30						

Impatience can rob us of opportunities to grow in our faith. The next time you feel impatience rising up in you, ask God, "What would You like me to learn while I wait?"

to-do list

- [ ]
- [ ]
- [ ]
- [ ]
- [ ]
- [ ]
- [ ]
- [ ]
- [ ]
- [ ]
- [ ]
- [ ]
- [ ]
- [ ]
- [ ]
- [ ]
- [ ]
- [ ]

SUNDAY, JUNE 2

MONDAY, JUNE 3

TUESDAY, JUNE 4

WEDNESDAY, JUNE 5

THURSDAY, JUNE 6

FRIDAY, JUNE 7

SATURDAY, JUNE 8

to-do list

☐
☐
☐
☐
☐
☐
☐
☐
☐
☐
☐
☐
☐
☐
☐
☐
☐

*Let patience have
its perfect work,
that you may be
perfect and complete,
lacking nothing.*

JAMES 1:4 NKJV

JUNE 2024

S	M	T	W	T	F	S
						1
2	3	4	5	6	7	8
9	10	11	12	13	14	15
16	17	18	19	20	21	22
23	24	25	26	27	28	29
30						

The peace between you and God is more than an agreement. It's the rebirth of a relationship. This peace is permanent, based on unconditional love.

to-do list

- [ ] ....
- [ ] ....
- [ ] ....
- [ ] ....
- [ ] ....
- [ ] ....
- [ ] ....
- [ ] ....
- [ ] ....
- [ ] ....
- [ ] ....
- [ ] ....
- [ ] ....
- [ ] ....
- [ ] ....
- [ ] ....
- [ ] ....
- [ ] ....

SUNDAY, JUNE 9

MONDAY, JUNE 10

TUESDAY, JUNE 11

WEDNESDAY, JUNE 12

THURSDAY, JUNE 13

FRIDAY, JUNE 14   *Flag Day*

SATURDAY, JUNE 15

- [ ]
- [ ]
- [ ]
- [ ]
- [ ]
- [ ]
- [ ]
- [ ]
- [ ]
- [ ]
- [ ]
- [ ]
- [ ]
- [ ]

Since we have been made right in God's sight by faith, we have peace with God because of what Jesus Christ our Lord has done for us.

ROMANS 5:1 NLT

JUNE 2024

S	M	T	W	T	F	S
						1
2	3	4	5	6	7	8
9	10	11	12	13	14	15
16	17	18	19	20	21	22
23	24	25	26	27	28	29
30						

To keep moving forward, run the race of faith one step at a time. Consider each day a fresh starting line. Moment by moment, with God's help, you will persevere.

to-do list

- [ ]
- [ ]
- [ ]
- [ ]
- [ ]
- [ ]
- [ ]
- [ ]
- [ ]
- [ ]
- [ ]
- [ ]
- [ ]
- [ ]
- [ ]
- [ ]
- [ ]

SUNDAY, JUNE 16 *Father's Day*

MONDAY, JUNE 17

TUESDAY, JUNE 18

WEDNESDAY, JUNE 19

THURSDAY, JUNE 20 *First Day of Summer*

FRIDAY, JUNE 21

SATURDAY, JUNE 22

to-do list

- [ ]
- [ ]
- [ ]
- [ ]
- [ ]
- [ ]
- [ ]
- [ ]
- [ ]
- [ ]
- [ ]
- [ ]
- [ ]
- [ ]
- [ ]
- [ ]

I have fought the good fight, I have finished the race, I have kept the faith.

2 TIMOTHY 4:7 NKJV

JUNE 2024

S	M	T	W	T	F	S
						1
2	3	4	5	6	7	8
9	10	11	12	13	14	15
16	17	18	19	20	21	22
23	24	25	26	27	28	29
30						

The more you grow in your faith, the more God will stretch your idea of who you are—and what you can do. Through God's power, you can confidently say, "Yes!" to doing anything He asks.

to-do list

- [ ]
- [ ]
- [ ]
- [ ]
- [ ]
- [ ]
- [ ]
- [ ]
- [ ]
- [ ]
- [ ]
- [ ]
- [ ]
- [ ]
- [ ]
- [ ]
- [ ]
- [ ]
- [ ]

SUNDAY, JUNE 23

MONDAY, JUNE 24

TUESDAY, JUNE 25

WEDNESDAY, JUNE 26

....

....

....

....

....

THURSDAY, JUNE 27

....

....

....

....

....

FRIDAY, JUNE 28

....

....

....

....

....

SATURDAY, JUNE 29

....

....

....

....

....

to-do list

- [ ]
- [ ]
- [ ]
- [ ]
- [ ]
- [ ]
- [ ]
- [ ]
- [ ]
- [ ]
- [ ]
- [ ]
- [ ]
- [ ]
- [ ]
- [ ]

We pray for God's power to help you do all the good things you hope to do and your faith makes you want to do.

2 THESSALONIANS 1:11 CEV

JULY 2024

SUNDAY	MONDAY	TUESDAY	WEDNESDAY
30	1	2	3
7	8	9	10
14	15	16	17
21	22	23	24
28	29	30	31

THURSDAY	FRIDAY	SATURDAY
4 *Independence Day*	5	6
11	12	13
18	19	20
25	26	27
1	2	3

....
....
....
....
....
....
....
....
....
....
....
....
....
....
....

JUNE

S	M	T	W	T	F	S
						1
2	3	4	5	7	7	8
9	10	11	12	13	14	15
16	17	18	19	20	21	22
23	24	25	26	27	28	29
30						

AUGUST

S	M	T	W	T	F	S
				1	2	3
4	5	6	7	8	9	10
11	12	13	14	15	16	17
18	19	20	21	22	23	24
25	26	27	28	29	30	31

Key to Freedom

Imagine being locked in prison for years. You're guilty, hopeless, helpless. Then, a beloved friend volunteers to take your place. You're set free as another woman takes your punishment as her own. How much do you value the cost of your freedom? In essence, this is what Christ did for you. When you place your faith in Him, you're handed the key to freedom. Honor Jesus' gift by living a life worthy of such sacrifice.

Goals *for the* Month

....

....

....

....

....

....

....

....

....

....

....

....

....

*The Scriptures declare that we are all
prisoners of sin, so we receive God's promise of
freedom only by believing in Jesus Christ.*

GALATIANS 3:22 NLT

JULY
2024

S	M	T	W	T	F	S
	1	2	3	4	5	6
7	8	9	10	11	12	13
14	15	16	17	18	19	20
21	22	23	24	25	26	27
28	29	30	31			

It's God's power working through you that allows you to accomplish more than you can on your own. Staying connected with God through prayer, obedience, reading the Bible, and loving others well will keep His power flowing freely into your life—and out into the world.

to-do list

- [ ] ....
- [ ] ....
- [ ] ....
- [ ] ....
- [ ] ....
- [ ] ....
- [ ] ....
- [ ] ....
- [ ] ....
- [ ] ....
- [ ] ....
- [ ] ....
- [ ] ....
- [ ] ....
- [ ] ....
- [ ] ....
- [ ] ....

SUNDAY, JUNE 30

MONDAY, JULY 1

TUESDAY, JULY 2

WEDNESDAY, JULY 3

....
....
....
....
....

THURSDAY, JULY 4   *Independence Day*

....
....
....
....
....

FRIDAY, JULY 5

....
....
....
....
....

SATURDAY, JULY 6

....
....
....
....
....

to-do list

☐
☐
☐
☐
☐
☐
☐
☐
☐
☐
☐
☐
☐
☐
☐
☐

We are like clay jars in which this treasure is stored. The real power comes from God and not from us.

2 CORINTHIANS 4:7 CEV

JULY 2024

S	M	T	W	T	F	S
	1	2	3	4	5	6
7	8	9	10	11	12	13
14	15	16	17	18	19	20
21	22	23	24	25	26	27
28	29	30	31			

The more frequently you pray, the easier it is to recognize God's voice. So, keep talking. God's listening. With time, you'll learn how to listen in return.

to-do list

- [ ]
- [ ]
- [ ]
- [ ]
- [ ]
- [ ]
- [ ]
- [ ]
- [ ]
- [ ]
- [ ]
- [ ]
- [ ]
- [ ]
- [ ]
- [ ]
- [ ]
- [ ]

SUNDAY, JULY 7

MONDAY, JULY 8

TUESDAY, JULY 9

WEDNESDAY, JULY 10

THURSDAY, JULY 11

FRIDAY, JULY 12

SATURDAY, JULY 13

to-do list

- [ ]
- [ ]
- [ ]
- [ ]
- [ ]
- [ ]
- [ ]
- [ ]
- [ ]
- [ ]
- [ ]
- [ ]
- [ ]
- [ ]
- [ ]
- [ ]

Be joyful in hope,
patient in affliction,
faithful in prayer.
ROMANS 12:12 NIV

JULY

2024

S	M	T	W	T	F	S
	1	2	3	4	5	6
7	8	9	10	11	12	13
14	15	16	17	18	19	20
21	22	23	24	25	26	27
28	29	30	31			

If we believe God loves us, believe Jesus is who He said He was, believe God has a plan for our lives, believe He's good, wise, and just—our prayers will reflect these beliefs. They'll be in line with God's will—with what God desires for our life.

to-do list

- ☐
- ☐
- ☐
- ☐
- ☐
- ☐
- ☐
- ☐
- ☐
- ☐
- ☐
- ☐
- ☐
- ☐
- ☐
- ☐
- ☐
- ☐

SUNDAY, JULY 14

MONDAY, JULY 15

TUESDAY, JULY 16

WEDNESDAY, JULY 17

....
....
....
....
....

THURSDAY, JULY 18

....
....
....
....
....

FRIDAY, JULY 19

....
....
....
....
....

SATURDAY, JULY 20

....
....
....
....
....

to-do list

- ☐
- ☐
- ☐
- ☐
- ☐
- ☐
- ☐
- ☐
- ☐
- ☐
- ☐
- ☐
- ☐
- ☐
- ☐
- ☐

*Everything you ask for
in prayer will be yours,
if you only have faith.*
MARK 11:24 CEV

JULY

2024

S	M	T	W	T	F	S
	1	2	3	4	5	6
7	8	9	10	11	12	13
14	15	16	17	18	19	20
21	22	23	24	25	26	27
28	29	30	31			

Breathe in and thank God for His gift of life. Then breathe out, asking Him to make you more aware of His hand at work in your life. Throughout the day, just breathe—drawing near to the one who gave you breath.

to-do list

- [ ]
- [ ]
- [ ]
- [ ]
- [ ]
- [ ]
- [ ]
- [ ]
- [ ]
- [ ]
- [ ]
- [ ]
- [ ]
- [ ]
- [ ]
- [ ]
- [ ]
- [ ]

SUNDAY, JULY 21

MONDAY, JULY 22

TUESDAY, JULY 23

WEDNESDAY, JULY 24

....

....

....

....

....

THURSDAY, JULY 25

....

....

....

....

....

FRIDAY, JULY 26

....

....

....

....

....

SATURDAY, JULY 27

....

....

....

....

....

to-do list

- [ ] ....
- [ ] ....
- [ ] ....
- [ ] ....
- [ ] ....
- [ ] ....
- [ ] ....
- [ ] ....
- [ ] ....
- [ ] ....
- [ ] ....
- [ ] ....
- [ ] ....
- [ ] ....
- [ ] ....
- [ ] ....
- [ ] ....

*I walk in the Lord's
presence as I live
here on earth!*
PSALM 116:9 NLT

AUGUST 2024

SUNDAY	MONDAY	TUESDAY	WEDNESDAY
28	29	30	31
4	5	6	7
11	12	13	14
18	19	20	21
25	26	27	28

THURSDAY	FRIDAY	SATURDAY
1	2	3
8	9	10
15	16	17
22	23	24
29	30	31

....

....

....

....

....

....

....

....

....

....

....

....

....

....

....

JULY

S	M	T	W	T	F	S
	1	2	3	4	5	6
7	8	9	10	11	12	13
14	15	16	17	18	19	20
21	22	23	24	25	26	27
28	29	30	31			

SEPTEMBER

S	M	T	W	T	F	S
1	2	3	4	5	6	7
8	9	10	11	12	13	14
15	16	17	18	19	20	21
22	23	24	25	26	27	28
29	30					

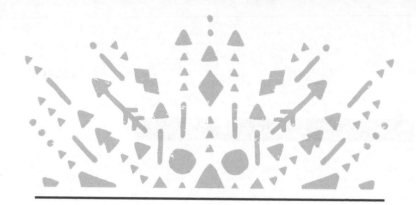

One Step at a Time

The future isn't something that's waiting off in the distance. It's right here, right now. Every breath you take brings you into that future, one step at a time. And the future that awaits you is good. Faith changes the course of your future as surely as it changes the landscape of your heart. God is preparing a home for you that will never be torn down, a place where your questions will be answered and your longings fulfilled.

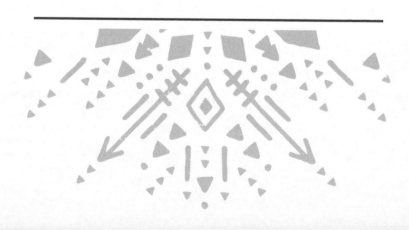

Goals *for the* Month

....

....

....

....

....

....

....

....

....

....

....

....

Because Jesus was raised from the dead,
we've been given a brand-new life and have
everything to live for, including a future in
heaven—and the future starts now!
1 PETER 1:3–4 MSG

AUGUST 2024

S	M	T	W	T	F	S
				1	2	3
4	5	6	7	8	9	10
11	12	13	14	15	16	17
18	19	20	21	22	23	24
25	26	27	28	29	30	31

Draw close to God in prayer. Never be afraid to enter His presence. You're always welcome, just as you are.

to-do list

- ☐ ....
- ☐ ....
- ☐ ....
- ☐ ....
- ☐ ....
- ☐ ....
- ☐ ....
- ☐ ....
- ☐ ....
- ☐ ....
- ☐ ....
- ☐ ....
- ☐ ....
- ☐ ....
- ☐ ....
- ☐ ....
- ☐ ....
- ☐ ....

SUNDAY, JULY 28

MONDAY, JULY 29

TUESDAY, JULY 30

WEDNESDAY, JULY 31

....
....
....
....
....

THURSDAY, AUGUST 1

....
....
....
....
....

FRIDAY, AUGUST 2

....
....
....
....
....

SATURDAY, AUGUST 3

....
....
....
....
....

to-do list

- [ ]
- [ ]
- [ ]
- [ ]
- [ ]
- [ ]
- [ ]
- [ ]
- [ ]
- [ ]
- [ ]
- [ ]
- [ ]
- [ ]
- [ ]
- [ ]

Because of Christ and our faith in him, we can now come boldly and confidently into God's presence.

EPHESIANS 3:12 NLT

AUGUST
2024

S	M	T	W	T	F	S
				1	2	3
4	5	6	7	8	9	10
11	12	13	14	15	16	17
18	19	20	21	22	23	24
25	26	27	28	29	30	31

Each day, ask God to help you live and love in a way that makes Him proud. Then, watch Him provide what you need to do what He asks.

to-do list

☐
☐
☐
☐
☐
☐
☐
☐
☐
☐
☐
☐
☐
☐
☐
☐
☐
☐

SUNDAY, AUGUST 4

MONDAY, AUGUST 5

TUESDAY, AUGUST 6

WEDNESDAY, AUGUST 7

THURSDAY, AUGUST 8

FRIDAY, AUGUST 9

SATURDAY, AUGUST 10

to-do list

☐
☐
☐
☐
☐
☐
☐
☐
☐
☐
☐
☐
☐
☐
☐
☐

"Seek the Kingdom of God above all else, and live righteously, and he will give you everything you need."

MATTHEW 6:33 NLT

AUGUST 2024

S	M	T	W	T	F	S
				1	2	3
4	5	6	7	8	9	10
11	12	13	14	15	16	17
18	19	20	21	22	23	24
25	26	27	28	29	30	31

What's God's priority for you? That you live a life of love and integrity. Keep these two things in mind as you decide what to add and remove from your schedule this week.

to-do list

- [ ]
- [ ]
- [ ]
- [ ]
- [ ]
- [ ]
- [ ]
- [ ]
- [ ]
- [ ]
- [ ]
- [ ]
- [ ]
- [ ]
- [ ]
- [ ]
- [ ]
- [ ]

SUNDAY, AUGUST 11

MONDAY, AUGUST 12

TUESDAY, AUGUST 13

WEDNESDAY, AUGUST 14

THURSDAY, AUGUST 15

FRIDAY, AUGUST 16

SATURDAY, AUGUST 17

to-do list

*Honor Christ and
put others first.*
EPHESIANS 5:21 CEV

AUGUST
2024

S	M	T	W	T	F	S
				1	2	3
4	5	6	7	8	9	10
11	12	13	14	15	16	17
18	19	20	21	22	23	24
25	26	27	28	29	30	31

The Bible says you'll face all kinds of storms in this life. But God's your safe place, regardless of what's raging all around you. He's with you in every storm, offering protection and peace. Don't hesitate to draw near.

to-do list

- ☐
- ☐
- ☐
- ☐
- ☐
- ☐
- ☐
- ☐
- ☐
- ☐
- ☐
- ☐
- ☐
- ☐
- ☐
- ☐
- ☐
- ☐

SUNDAY, AUGUST 18

MONDAY, AUGUST 19

TUESDAY, AUGUST 20

WEDNESDAY, AUGUST 21

....
....
....
....
....

THURSDAY, AUGUST 22

....
....
....
....
....

FRIDAY, AUGUST 23

....
....
....
....
....

SATURDAY, AUGUST 24

....
....
....
....
....

to-do list

.... ☐
.... ☐
.... ☐
.... ☐
.... ☐
.... ☐
.... ☐
.... ☐
.... ☐
.... ☐
.... ☐
.... ☐
.... ☐
.... ☐
.... ☐

GOD's a safe-house for the battered, a sanctuary during bad times. The moment you arrive, you relax; you're never sorry you knocked.

PSALM 9:9–10 MSG

AUGUST

2024

S	M	T	W	T	F	S
				1	2	3
4	5	6	7	8	9	10
11	12	13	14	15	16	17
18	19	20	21	22	23	24
25	26	27	28	29	30	31

When God says He'll provide what we need, it's always on His terms, not ours. He provides everything we need to do everything He's asked us to do.

to-do list

- ☐ ....
- ☐ ....
- ☐ ....
- ☐ ....
- ☐ ....
- ☐ ....
- ☐ ....
- ☐ ....
- ☐ ....
- ☐ ....
- ☐ ....
- ☐ ....
- ☐ ....
- ☐ ....
- ☐ ....
- ☐ ....
- ☐ ....

SUNDAY, AUGUST 25

MONDAY, AUGUST 26

TUESDAY, AUGUST 27

WEDNESDAY, AUGUST 28

THURSDAY, AUGUST 29

FRIDAY, AUGUST 30

SATURDAY, AUGUST 31

to-do list

- [ ]
- [ ]
- [ ]
- [ ]
- [ ]
- [ ]
- [ ]
- [ ]
- [ ]
- [ ]
- [ ]
- [ ]
- [ ]
- [ ]
- [ ]

*God will generously
provide all you need.
Then you will always
have everything you
need and plenty left over
to share with others.*

2 CORINTHIANS 9:8 NLT

SEPTEMBER 2024

SUNDAY	MONDAY	TUESDAY	WEDNESDAY
1	2	3	4
	Labor Day		
8	9	10	11
15	16	17	18
22	23	24	25
First Day of Autumn			
29	30	1	2

THURSDAY	FRIDAY	SATURDAY
5	6	7
12	13	14
19	20	21
26	27	28
3	4	5

....
....
....
....
....
....
....
....
....
....
....
....
....
....

AUGUST

S	M	T	W	T	F	S
				1	2	3
4	5	6	7	8	9	10
11	12	13	14	15	16	17
18	19	20	21	22	23	24
25	26	27	28	29	30	31

OCTOBER

S	M	T	W	T	F	S
		1	2	3	4	5
6	7	8	9	10	11	12
13	14	15	16	17	18	19
20	21	22	23	24	25	26
27	28	29	30	31		

More Reasons to Hope

What do you hope for? *Really* hope for? Perhaps it's security, significance, or a relationship that will never let you down. Hopes like these are fulfilled solely through faith. Read God's track record as recorded in the Bible. He keeps His promises in areas like these time and again. It's true that it takes faith to place your hope in someone you can't see. But you're building your own track record with God. Day by day, you'll discover more reasons to hope in Him.

Goals *for the* Month

....

....

....

....

....

....

....

....

....

....

....

....

....

....

*Let us hold unswervingly to the hope we
profess, for he who promised is faithful.*
HEBREWS 10:23 NIV

SEPTEMBER
2024

S	M	T	W	T	F	S
1	2	3	4	5	6	7
8	9	10	11	12	13	14
15	16	17	18	19	20	21
22	23	24	25	26	27	28
29	30					

Faith provides a singular purpose for living: to love God and others. Fulfilling this purpose requires living prayerfully and with intention. This week, ask God to help slow you down. Consider your true purpose as you make your plans.

to-do list

☐
☐
☐
☐
☐
☐
☐
☐
☐
☐
☐
☐
☐
☐
☐
☐
☐
☐

SUNDAY, SEPTEMBER 1

MONDAY, SEPTEMBER 2 *Labor Day*

TUESDAY, SEPTEMBER 3

WEDNESDAY, SEPTEMBER 4

....
....
....
....
....

THURSDAY, SEPTEMBER 5

....
....
....
....
....

FRIDAY, SEPTEMBER 6

....
....
....
....
....

SATURDAY, SEPTEMBER 7

....
....
....
....
....

to-do list

- [ ]
- [ ]
- [ ]
- [ ]
- [ ]
- [ ]
- [ ]
- [ ]
- [ ]
- [ ]
- [ ]
- [ ]
- [ ]
- [ ]
- [ ]
- [ ]

*Now the purpose of the
commandment is love
from a pure heart, from
a good conscience, and
from sincere faith.*

1 TIMOTHY 1:5 NKJV

SEPTEMBER
2024

S	M	T	W	T	F	S
1	2	3	4	5	6	7
8	9	10	11	12	13	14
15	16	17	18	19	20	21
22	23	24	25	26	27	28
29	30					

As a woman of faith, you've accepted God as the ultimate authority figure over you. God's love tempers the power of His position. Respecting Him is just one more way of worshipping Him.

to-do list

- ☐
- ☐
- ☐
- ☐
- ☐
- ☐
- ☐
- ☐
- ☐
- ☐
- ☐
- ☐
- ☐
- ☐
- ☐
- ☐
- ☐

SUNDAY, SEPTEMBER 8

MONDAY, SEPTEMBER 9

TUESDAY, SEPTEMBER 10

WEDNESDAY, SEPTEMBER 11

....

....

....

....

....

THURSDAY, SEPTEMBER 12

....

....

....

....

....

FRIDAY, SEPTEMBER 13

....

....

....

....

....

SATURDAY, SEPTEMBER 14

....

....

....

....

....

to-do list

☐
☐
☐
☐
☐
☐
☐
☐
☐
☐
☐
☐
☐
☐
☐
☐
☐

Everything you were taught can be put into a few words: Respect and obey God! This is what life is all about.

ECCLESIASTES 12:13 CEV

SEPTEMBER
2024

S	M	T	W	T	F	S
1	2	3	4	5	6	7
8	9	10	11	12	13	14
15	16	17	18	19	20	21
22	23	24	25	26	27	28
29	30					

Faith is not a to-do list of assignments
from God. It's an invitation to relationship.
It's about getting to know who God is
and who He created you to be. It's about
resting in God's love and acceptance.

to-do list

- [ ] ....
- [ ] ....
- [ ] ....
- [ ] ....
- [ ] ....
- [ ] ....
- [ ] ....
- [ ] ....
- [ ] ....
- [ ] ....
- [ ] ....
- [ ] ....
- [ ] ....
- [ ] ....
- [ ] ....
- [ ] ....
- [ ] ....

SUNDAY, SEPTEMBER 15

MONDAY, SEPTEMBER 16

TUESDAY, SEPTEMBER 17

WEDNESDAY, SEPTEMBER 18

THURSDAY, SEPTEMBER 19

FRIDAY, SEPTEMBER 20

SATURDAY, SEPTEMBER 21

to-do list

- [ ]
- [ ]
- [ ]
- [ ]
- [ ]
- [ ]
- [ ]
- [ ]
- [ ]
- [ ]
- [ ]
- [ ]
- [ ]
- [ ]

"Are you tired? Worn out? Burned out on religion? Come to me. Get away with me and you'll recover your life. I'll show you how to take a real rest."

MATTHEW 11:28–29 MSG

SEPTEMBER
2024

S	M	T	W	T	F	S
1	2	3	4	5	6	7
8	9	10	11	12	13	14
15	16	17	18	19	20	21
22	23	24	25	26	27	28
29	30					

You have many important roles to fill in this life. Rest is one of God's gifts that can empower you to accomplish what He's given you to do.

to-do list

- [ ]
- [ ]
- [ ]
- [ ]
- [ ]
- [ ]
- [ ]
- [ ]
- [ ]
- [ ]
- [ ]
- [ ]
- [ ]
- [ ]
- [ ]
- [ ]

SUNDAY, SEPTEMBER 22   *First Day of Autumn*

MONDAY, SEPTEMBER 23

TUESDAY, SEPTEMBER 24

WEDNESDAY, SEPTEMBER 25

THURSDAY, SEPTEMBER 26

FRIDAY, SEPTEMBER 27

SATURDAY, SEPTEMBER 28

to-do list

☐
☐
☐
☐
☐
☐
☐
☐
☐
☐
☐
☐
☐

*It is useless for you
to work so hard from
early morning until
late at night, anxiously
working for food to
eat; for God gives rest
to his loved ones.*

PSALM 127:2 NLT

OCTOBER 2024

SUNDAY	MONDAY	TUESDAY	WEDNESDAY
29	30	1	2
6	7	8	9
13	14 *Columbus Day*	15	16
20	21	22	23
27	28	29	30

THURSDAY	FRIDAY	SATURDAY
3	4	5
10	11	12
17	18	19
24	25	26
31 *Halloween*	1	2

SEPTEMBER

S	M	T	W	T	F	S
1	2	3	4	5	6	7
8	9	10	11	12	13	14
15	16	17	18	19	20	21
22	23	24	25	26	27	28
29	30					

NOVEMBER

S	M	T	W	T	F	S
					1	2
3	4	5	6	7	8	9
10	11	12	13	14	15	16
17	18	19	20	21	22	23
24	25	26	27	28	29	30

Incredible Potential

Your life has incredible potential. It's filled with opportunities to love, laugh, learn, and make a positive difference in this world. Faith turns every opportunity into an invitation: Will you choose to live this moment in a way that honors God? What you do with your life matters. But, ultimately, who you become is more important than what you accomplish. As your faith grows, your heart more resembles God's own. That's when you recognize where your true potential lies.

Goals *for the* Month

....
....
....
....
....
....
....
....
....
....
....
....
....
....
....

*As obedient children, let yourselves be pulled
into a way of life shaped by God's life, a life
energetic and blazing with holiness.*

1 PETER 1:15 MSG

OCTOBER

2024

S	M	T	W	T	F	S
		1	2	3	4	5
6	7	8	9	10	11	12
13	14	15	16	17	18	19
20	21	22	23	24	25	26
27	28	29	30	31		

Anytime you stumble, go straight to God. Confess what you've done. You can trust it's forgiven *and* forgotten.

to-do list

- ☐ ....
- ☐ ....
- ☐ ....
- ☐ ....
- ☐ ....
- ☐ ....
- ☐ ....
- ☐ ....
- ☐ ....
- ☐ ....
- ☐ ....
- ☐ ....
- ☐ ....
- ☐ ....
- ☐ ....
- ☐ ....
- ☐ ....
- ☐ ....

SUNDAY, SEPTEMBER 29

MONDAY, SEPTEMBER 30

TUESDAY, OCTOBER 1

WEDNESDAY, OCTOBER 2

....
....
....
....
....

THURSDAY, OCTOBER 3

....
....
....
....
....

FRIDAY, OCTOBER 4

....
....
....
....
....

SATURDAY, OCTOBER 5

....
....
....
....
....

to-do list

- [ ]
- [ ]
- [ ]
- [ ]
- [ ]
- [ ]
- [ ]
- [ ]
- [ ]
- [ ]
- [ ]
- [ ]
- [ ]
- [ ]
- [ ]
- [ ]

*God, in his grace,
freely makes us right
in his sight. He did this
through Christ Jesus
when he freed us from
the penalty for our sins.*

ROMANS 3:24 NLT

OCTOBER

2024

S	M	T	W	T	F	S
		1	2	3	4	5
6	7	8	9	10	11	12
13	14	15	16	17	18	19
20	21	22	23	24	25	26
27	28	29	30	31		

Choosing to follow Jesus will involve sacrifice on your part. Allow Him to show you how sacrifice can lead to something good.

to-do list

☐
☐
☐
☐
☐
☐
☐
☐
☐
☐
☐
☐
☐
☐
☐
☐
☐

SUNDAY, OCTOBER 6

MONDAY, OCTOBER 7

TUESDAY, OCTOBER 8

WEDNESDAY, OCTOBER 9

THURSDAY, OCTOBER 10

FRIDAY, OCTOBER 11

SATURDAY, OCTOBER 12

to-do list

- [ ]
- [ ]
- [ ]
- [ ]
- [ ]
- [ ]
- [ ]
- [ ]
- [ ]
- [ ]
- [ ]
- [ ]
- [ ]
- [ ]
- [ ]
- [ ]

God sent Christ to be our sacrifice. Christ offered his life's blood, so that by faith in him we could come to God.

ROMANS 3:25 CEV

OCTOBER
2024

S	M	T	W	T	F	S
		1	2	3	4	5
6	7	8	9	10	11	12
13	14	15	16	17	18	19
20	21	22	23	24	25	26
27	28	29	30	31		

Jesus saved you because you took hold of His hand in faith when He offered to pull you from the waves. Without Him, you were lost. Now, you're found—saved and secure.

to-do list

- [ ] ....
- [ ] ....
- [ ] ....
- [ ] ....
- [ ] ....
- [ ] ....
- [ ] ....
- [ ] ....
- [ ] ....
- [ ] ....
- [ ] ....
- [ ] ....
- [ ] ....
- [ ] ....
- [ ] ....
- [ ] ....
- [ ] ....
- [ ] ....

SUNDAY, OCTOBER 13

MONDAY, OCTOBER 14   *Columbus Day*

TUESDAY, OCTOBER 15

WEDNESDAY, OCTOBER 16

THURSDAY, OCTOBER 17

FRIDAY, OCTOBER 18

SATURDAY, OCTOBER 19

to-do list

☐
☐
☐
☐
☐
☐
☐
☐
☐
☐
☐
☐
☐
☐
☐
☐
☐

Salvation is not a reward for the good things we have done, so none of us can boast about it.

EPHESIANS 2:9 NLT

OCTOBER
2024

S	M	T	W	T	F	S
		1	2	3	4	5
6	7	8	9	10	11	12
13	14	15	16	17	18	19
20	21	22	23	24	25	26
27	28	29	30	31		

God's love, His character, His gift of salvation, and every promise He's ever made to you stands firm, immovable. You can lean on Him in any and every circumstance, secure in the fact that He'll never let you down.

to-do list

☐
☐
☐
☐
☐
☐
☐
☐
☐
☐
☐
☐
☐
☐
☐
☐
☐
☐

SUNDAY, OCTOBER 20

MONDAY, OCTOBER 21

TUESDAY, OCTOBER 22

WEDNESDAY, OCTOBER 23

THURSDAY, OCTOBER 24

FRIDAY, OCTOBER 25

SATURDAY, OCTOBER 26

to-do list

☐
☐
☐
☐
☐
☐
☐
☐
☐
☐
☐
☐
☐
☐
☐
☐
☐

I am sure that nothing can separate us from God's love—not life or death, not angels or spirits, not the present or the future.

ROMANS 8:38 CEV

NOVEMBER 2024

SUNDAY	MONDAY	TUESDAY	WEDNESDAY
27	28	29	30
3 *Daylight Saving Time Ends*	4	5 *Election Day*	6
10	11 *Veterans Day*	12	13
17	18	19	20
24	25	26	27

THURSDAY	FRIDAY	SATURDAY
31	1	2
7	8	9
14	15	16
21	22	23
28	29	30
Thanksgiving Day		

OCTOBER

S	M	T	W	T	F	S
		1	2	3	4	5
6	7	8	9	10	11	12
13	14	15	16	17	18	19
20	21	22	23	24	25	26
27	28	29	30	31		

DECEMBER

S	M	T	W	T	F	S
1	2	3	4	5	6	7
8	9	10	11	12	13	14
15	16	17	18	19	20	21
22	23	24	25	26	27	28
29	30	31				

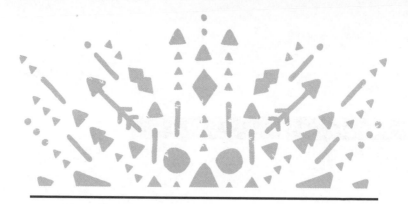

Aware of the Details

It takes faith, and science, to appreciate the wonders of nature. Science describes the improbability of generations of butterflies migrating thousands of miles to specific destinations they've never experienced firsthand or the impossibly delicate balance of our orbiting solar system. Faith assures us God not only understands miracles like these but sets them in motion. Surely, a God who cares for the tiniest detail of nature, is aware—and at work—in every detail of your life.

Goals *for the* Month

....

....

....

....

....

....

....

....

....

....

....

....

....

*By faith we understand that the universe was
formed at God's command, so that what is seen
was not made out of what was visible.*

HEBREWS 11:3 NIV

NOVEMBER
2024

S	M	T	W	T	F	S
					1	2
3	4	5	6	7	8	9
10	11	12	13	14	15	16
17	18	19	20	21	22	23
24	25	26	27	28	29	30

Serving God isn't always an easy path.
You may not see the big picture behind
what you're asked to do. But you can
trust God's plan for you is good.

to-do list

- [ ]
- [ ]
- [ ]
- [ ]
- [ ]
- [ ]
- [ ]
- [ ]
- [ ]
- [ ]
- [ ]
- [ ]
- [ ]
- [ ]
- [ ]
- [ ]
- [ ]
- [ ]

SUNDAY, OCTOBER 27

MONDAY, OCTOBER 28

TUESDAY, OCTOBER 29

WEDNESDAY, OCTOBER 30

THURSDAY, OCTOBER 31 *Halloween*

FRIDAY, NOVEMBER 1

SATURDAY, NOVEMBER 2

to-do list

☐
☐
☐
☐
☐
☐
☐
☐
☐
☐
☐
☐
☐
☐
☐
☐

*See how Abraham's
faith and deeds worked
together. He proved
his faith was real
by what he did.*

JAMES 2:22 CEV

NOVEMBER
2024

S	M	T	W	T	F	S
					1	2
3	4	5	6	7	8	9
10	11	12	13	14	15	16
17	18	19	20	21	22	23
24	25	26	27	28	29	30

Be honest. Tell God how you feel. He loves you like a father, friend, lover, husband, and deliverer. Walk with Him. He'll lead you toward healing and wholeness.

to-do list

- [ ]
- [ ]
- [ ]
- [ ]
- [ ]
- [ ]
- [ ]
- [ ]
- [ ]
- [ ]
- [ ]
- [ ]
- [ ]
- [ ]
- [ ]
- [ ]
- [ ]
- [ ]

SUNDAY, NOVEMBER 3
Daylight Saving Time Ends

MONDAY, NOVEMBER 4

TUESDAY, NOVEMBER 5
Election Day

WEDNESDAY, NOVEMBER 6

THURSDAY, NOVEMBER 7

FRIDAY, NOVEMBER 8

SATURDAY, NOVEMBER 9

to-do list

- [ ]
- [ ]
- [ ]
- [ ]
- [ ]
- [ ]
- [ ]
- [ ]
- [ ]
- [ ]
- [ ]
- [ ]
- [ ]
- [ ]

*The LORD All-Powerful,
the Holy God of Israel,
rules all the earth.
He is your Creator
and husband, and
he will rescue you.*

ISAIAH 54:5 CEV

NOVEMBER
2024

S	M	T	W	T	F	S
					1	2
3	4	5	6	7	8	9
10	11	12	13	14	15	16
17	18	19	20	21	22	23
24	25	26	27	28	29	30

The Bible reminds us that our words have power. We're responsible for how we use that power. Will we hurt or heal? Build up or tear down? Allow faith to help you choose wisely.

to-do list

- ☐
- ☐
- ☐
- ☐
- ☐
- ☐
- ☐
- ☐
- ☐
- ☐
- ☐
- ☐
- ☐
- ☐
- ☐
- ☐
- ☐

SUNDAY, NOVEMBER 10

MONDAY, NOVEMBER 11   *Veterans Day*

TUESDAY, NOVEMBER 12

WEDNESDAY, NOVEMBER 13

....

....

....

....

....

THURSDAY, NOVEMBER 14

....

....

....

....

....

FRIDAY, NOVEMBER 15

....

....

....

....

....

SATURDAY, NOVEMBER 16

....

....

....

....

....

to-do list

- [ ] ....
- [ ] ....
- [ ] ....
- [ ] ....
- [ ] ....
- [ ] ....
- [ ] ....
- [ ] ....
- [ ] ....
- [ ] ....
- [ ] ....
- [ ] ....
- [ ] ....
- [ ] ....
- [ ] ....
- [ ] ....

Let everything you say be good and helpful, so that your words will be an encouragement to those who hear them.

EPHESIANS 4:29 NLT

NOVEMBER 2024

S	M	T	W	T	F	S
					1	2
3	4	5	6	7	8	9
10	11	12	13	14	15	16
17	18	19	20	21	22	23
24	25	26	27	28	29	30

The more time you spend with God, the more your character will begin to resemble His—and the more humble you'll be in His presence. This is exactly the kind of woman God's looking for to do wonderful things in this world.

to-do list

- ☐
- ☐
- ☐
- ☐
- ☐
- ☐
- ☐
- ☐
- ☐
- ☐
- ☐
- ☐
- ☐
- ☐
- ☐
- ☐
- ☐

SUNDAY, NOVEMBER 17

MONDAY, NOVEMBER 18

TUESDAY, NOVEMBER 19

WEDNESDAY, NOVEMBER 20

....
....
....
....
....

THURSDAY, NOVEMBER 21

....
....
....
....
....

FRIDAY, NOVEMBER 22

....
....
....
....
....

SATURDAY, NOVEMBER 23

....
....
....
....
....

to-do list

☐
☐
☐
☐
☐
☐
☐
☐
☐
☐
☐
☐
☐
☐
☐
☐
☐

*The godly will flourish
like palm trees.... Even
in old age they will still
produce fruit; they will
remain vital and green.*

PSALM 92:12, 14 NLT

NOVEMBER
2024

S	M	T	W	T	F	S
					1	2
3	4	5	6	7	8	9
10	11	12	13	14	15	16
17	18	19	20	21	22	23
24	25	26	27	28	29	30

When God reveals a weed budding in your character, pull it up by the roots. A fresh sprout of love? Water it regularly with kindness and sacrifice. Tend to your spiritual growth each day, and beautiful things will begin to take root.

to-do list

- [ ]
- [ ]
- [ ]
- [ ]
- [ ]
- [ ]
- [ ]
- [ ]
- [ ]
- [ ]
- [ ]
- [ ]
- [ ]
- [ ]
- [ ]
- [ ]
- [ ]
- [ ]

SUNDAY, NOVEMBER 24

MONDAY, NOVEMBER 25

TUESDAY, NOVEMBER 26

WEDNESDAY, NOVEMBER 27

....
....
....
....
....

THURSDAY, NOVEMBER 28   *Thanksgiving Day*

....
....
....
....
....

FRIDAY, NOVEMBER 29

....
....
....
....
....

SATURDAY, NOVEMBER 30

....
....
....
....
....

to-do list

- [ ] ....
- [ ] ....
- [ ] ....
- [ ] ....
- [ ] ....
- [ ] ....
- [ ] ....
- [ ] ....
- [ ] ....
- [ ] ....
- [ ] ....
- [ ] ....
- [ ] ....
- [ ] ....
- [ ] ....

*Do your best to improve
your faith by adding
goodness, understanding,
self-control, patience,
devotion to God, concern
for others, and love.*

2 PETER 1:5–7 CEV

DECEMBER 2024

SUNDAY	MONDAY	TUESDAY	WEDNESDAY
1	2	3	4
8	9	10	11
15	16	17	18
22	23	24 *Christmas Eve*	25 *Christmas Day* *Hanukkah Begins at Sundown*
29	30	31 *New Year's Eve*	1

THURSDAY	FRIDAY	SATURDAY
5	6	7
12	13	14
19	20	21 First Day of Winter
26	27	28
2	3	4

NOVEMBER

S	M	T	W	T	F	S
					1	2
3	4	5	6	7	8	9
10	11	12	13	14	15	16
17	18	19	20	21	22	23
24	25	26	27	28	29	30

JANUARY

S	M	T	W	T	F	S
			1	2	3	4
5	6	7	8	9	10	11
12	13	14	15	16	17	18
19	20	21	22	23	24	25
26	27	28	29	30	31	

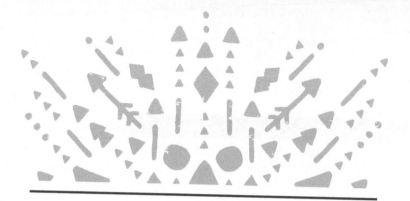

A Written Invitation

God's story is written in more places than the Bible. It's written in the glory of the setting sun, the faithfulness of the ocean tides, the symphony of a thunderstorm, and the detail of a dragonfly's wing. It's written in every cell of you. Take time to "read" more about who God is as described through His creation. Contemplate His organizational skills, creative genius, and love of diversity. Consider nature God's written invitation to worship and wonder.

Goals *for the* Month

....
....
....
....
....
....
....
....
....
....
....
....

*Ever since the world was created, people have
seen the earth and sky. Through everything
God made, they can clearly see his invisible
qualities—his eternal power and divine nature.*

ROMANS 1:20 NLT

DECEMBER
2024

S	M	T	W	T	F	S
1	2	3	4	5	6	7
8	9	10	11	12	13	14
15	16	17	18	19	20	21
22	23	24	25	26	27	28
29	30	31				

Committing whatever you do to God isn't asking Him to bless what you've already decided to do. It's inviting Him into the planning process. Make sure your dreams and goals are in line with God's. Then get to work— leaving the outcome in His hands.

to-do list

- [ ] ....
- [ ] ....
- [ ] ....
- [ ] ....
- [ ] ....
- [ ] ....
- [ ] ....
- [ ] ....
- [ ] ....
- [ ] ....
- [ ] ....
- [ ] ....
- [ ] ....
- [ ] ....
- [ ] ....
- [ ] ....
- [ ] ....
- [ ] ....

SUNDAY, DECEMBER 1

....
....
....
....
....

MONDAY, DECEMBER 2

....
....
....
....

TUESDAY, DECEMBER 3

....
....
....
....

WEDNESDAY, DECEMBER 4

THURSDAY, DECEMBER 5

FRIDAY, DECEMBER 6

SATURDAY, DECEMBER 7

to-do list

☐
☐
☐
☐
☐
☐
☐
☐
☐
☐
☐
☐
☐
☐
☐
☐

Commit to the LORD whatever you do, and he will establish your plans.

PROVERBS 16:3 NIV

DECEMBER

2024

S	M	T	W	T	F	S
1	2	3	4	5	6	7
8	9	10	11	12	13	14
15	16	17	18	19	20	21
22	23	24	25	26	27	28
29	30	31				

A successful life is made up of
successful days—and a truly successful
day is one that draws you closer
to God and His plans for you.

to-do list

- ☐ ....
- ☐ ....
- ☐ ....
- ☐ ....
- ☐ ....
- ☐ ....
- ☐ ....
- ☐ ....
- ☐ ....
- ☐ ....
- ☐ ....
- ☐ ....
- ☐ ....
- ☐ ....
- ☐ ....
- ☐ ....
- ☐ ....
- ☐ ....

SUNDAY, DECEMBER 8

MONDAY, DECEMBER 9

TUESDAY, DECEMBER 10

WEDNESDAY, DECEMBER 11

....

....

....

....

....

THURSDAY, DECEMBER 12

....

....

....

....

....

FRIDAY, DECEMBER 13

....

....

....

....

....

SATURDAY, DECEMBER 14

....

....

....

....

....

to-do list

- [ ]
- [ ]
- [ ]
- [ ]
- [ ]
- [ ]
- [ ]
- [ ]
- [ ]
- [ ]
- [ ]
- [ ]
- [ ]
- [ ]
- [ ]

"The market is flooded with surefire, easygoing formulas for a successful life.... The way to life—to God!—is vigorous and requires total attention."

MATTHEW 7:13–14 MSG

DECEMBER
2024

S	M	T	W	T	F	S
1	2	3	4	5	6	7
8	9	10	11	12	13	14
15	16	17	18	19	20	21
22	23	24	25	26	27	28
29	30	31				

You may not always understand the "whys" behind God's ways, but the more you risk trusting Him with the little things, the more confident you'll be entrusting Him with the big ones.

to-do list

- ☐
- ☐
- ☐
- ☐
- ☐
- ☐
- ☐
- ☐
- ☐
- ☐
- ☐
- ☐
- ☐
- ☐
- ☐
- ☐
- ☐
- ☐

SUNDAY, DECEMBER 15

MONDAY, DECEMBER 16

TUESDAY, DECEMBER 17

WEDNESDAY, DECEMBER 18

THURSDAY, DECEMBER 19

FRIDAY, DECEMBER 20

SATURDAY, DECEMBER 21   *First Day of Winter*

to-do list

☐
☐
☐
☐
☐
☐
☐
☐
☐
☐
☐
☐
☐
☐
☐
☐

*Trust in the LORD
with all your heart,
and lean not on your
own understanding.*

PROVERBS 3:5 NKJV

DECEMBER
2024

S	M	T	W	T	F	S
1	2	3	4	5	6	7
8	9	10	11	12	13	14
15	16	17	18	19	20	21
22	23	24	25	26	27	28
29	30	31				

As you grow in your faith, you'll grow to trust God's timing more and more. Expect Him to surprise you with the perfect harvest always delivered at exactly the right time.

to-do list

- [ ]
- [ ]
- [ ]
- [ ]
- [ ]
- [ ]
- [ ]
- [ ]
- [ ]
- [ ]
- [ ]
- [ ]
- [ ]
- [ ]
- [ ]
- [ ]
- [ ]

SUNDAY, DECEMBER 22

MONDAY, DECEMBER 23

TUESDAY, DECEMBER 24 *Christmas Eve*

WEDNESDAY, DECEMBER 25   *Christmas Day*
                         Hanukkah Begins at Sundown

THURSDAY, DECEMBER 26

FRIDAY, DECEMBER 27

SATURDAY, DECEMBER 28

to-do list

☐
☐
☐
☐
☐
☐
☐
☐
☐
☐
☐
☐
☐

The LORD longs to be gracious to you; therefore he will rise up to show you compassion. For the LORD is a God of justice. Blessed are all who wait for him!

ISAIAH 30:18 NIV

DECEMBER
2024

S	M	T	W	T	F	S
1	2	3	4	5	6	7
8	9	10	11	12	13	14
15	16	17	18	19	20	21
22	23	24	25	26	27	28
29	30	31				

Give yourself wholeheartedly to the task at hand, no matter how small. Give God your best by doing your best. He gave His best for you.

to-do list

- ☐ ....
- ☐ ....
- ☐ ....
- ☐ ....
- ☐ ....
- ☐ ....
- ☐ ....
- ☐ ....
- ☐ ....
- ☐ ....
- ☐ ....
- ☐ ....
- ☐ ....
- ☐ ....
- ☐ ....
- ☐ ....
- ☐ ....
- ☐ ....

SUNDAY, DECEMBER 29

MONDAY, DECEMBER 30

TUESDAY, DECEMBER 31   *New Year's Eve*

WEDNESDAY, JANUARY 1   *New Year's Day*

....

....

....

....

....

THURSDAY, JANUARY 2

....

....

....

....

....

FRIDAY, JANUARY 3

....

....

....

....

....

SATURDAY, JANUARY 4

....

....

....

....

....

to-do list

☐
☐
☐
☐
☐
☐
☐
☐
☐
☐
☐
☐
☐
☐
☐
☐

Whatever you say or do should be done in the name of the Lord Jesus, as you give thanks to God the Father because of him.

COLOSSIANS 3:17 CEV

CONTACTS

Name:

Address:

Phone: Mobile:

Email:

Name:

Address:

Phone: Mobile:

Email:

Name:

Address:

Phone: Mobile:

Email:

Name:

Address:

Phone: Mobile:

Email:

CONTACTS

Name:

Address:

Phone: Mobile:

Email:

Name:

Address:

Phone: Mobile:

Email:

Name:

Address:

Phone: Mobile:

Email:

Name:

Address:

Phone: Mobile:

Email:

CONTACTS

Name:

Address:

Phone: Mobile:

Email:

Name:

Address:

Phone: Mobile:

Email:

Name:

Address:

Phone: Mobile:

Email:

Name:

Address:

Phone: Mobile:

Email:

CONTACTS

Name:

Address:

Phone: Mobile:

Email:

Name:

Address:

Phone: Mobile:

Email:

Name:

Address:

Phone: Mobile:

Email:

Name:

Address:

Phone: Mobile:

Email:

CONTACTS

Name:

Address:

Phone: Mobile:

Email:

Name:

Address:

Phone: Mobile:

Email:

Name:

Address:

Phone: Mobile:

Email:

Name:

Address:

Phone: Mobile:

Email:

CONTACTS

Name:

Address:

Phone: Mobile:

Email:

Name:

Address:

Phone: Mobile:

Email:

Name:

Address:

Phone: Mobile:

Email:

Name:

Address:

Phone: Mobile:

Email:

CONTACTS

Name:

Address:

Phone: Mobile:

Email:

Name:

Address:

Phone: Mobile:

Email:

Name:

Address:

Phone: Mobile:

Email:

Name:

Address:

Phone: Mobile:

Email:

CONTACTS

Name:

Address:

Phone: Mobile:

Email:

Name:

Address:

Phone: Mobile:

Email:

Name:

Address:

Phone: Mobile:

Email:

Name:

Address:

Phone: Mobile:

Email:

CONTACTS

Name:

Address:

Phone: Mobile:

Email:

Name:

Address:

Phone: Mobile:

Email:

Name:

Address:

Phone: Mobile:

Email:

Name:

Address:

Phone: Mobile:

Email:

CONTACTS

Name:

Address:

Phone: Mobile:

Email:

Name:

Address:

Phone: Mobile:

Email:

Name:

Address:

Phone: Mobile:

Email:

Name:

Address:

Phone: Mobile:

Email:

CONTACTS

Name:

Address:

Phone: Mobile:

Email:

Name:

Address:

Phone: Mobile:

Email:

Name:

Address:

Phone: Mobile:

Email:

Name:

Address:

Phone: Mobile:

Email:

CONTACTS

Name:

Address:

Phone: Mobile:

Email:

Name:

Address:

Phone: Mobile:

Email:

Name:

Address:

Phone: Mobile:

Email:

Name:

Address:

Phone: Mobile:

Email:

CONTACTS

Name:

Address:

Phone: Mobile:

Email:

Name:

Address:

Phone: Mobile:

Email:

Name:

Address:

Phone: Mobile:

Email:

Name:

Address:

Phone: Mobile:

Email:

CONTACTS

Name:
....
Address:
....

....
Phone: Mobile:
....
Email:

Name:
....
Address:
....

....
Phone: Mobile:
....
Email:

Name:
....
Address:
....

....
Phone: Mobile:
....
Email:

Name:
....
Address:
....

....
Phone: Mobile:
....
Email:

2025

JANUARY
S	M	T	W	T	F	S
			1	2	3	4
5	6	7	8	9	10	11
12	13	14	15	16	17	18
19	20	21	22	23	24	25
26	27	28	29	30	31	

FEBRUARY
S	M	T	W	T	F	S
						1
2	3	4	5	6	7	8
9	10	11	12	13	14	15
16	17	18	19	20	21	22
23	24	25	26	27	28	

MARCH
S	M	T	W	T	F	S
						1
2	3	4	5	6	7	8
9	10	11	12	13	14	15
16	17	18	19	20	21	22
23	24	25	26	27	28	29
30	31					

APRIL
S	M	T	W	T	F	S
		1	2	3	4	5
6	7	8	9	10	11	12
13	14	15	16	17	18	19
20	21	22	23	24	25	26
27	28	29	30			

MAY
S	M	T	W	T	F	S
				1	2	3
4	5	6	7	8	9	10
11	12	13	14	15	16	17
18	19	20	21	22	23	24
25	26	27	28	29	30	31

JUNE
S	M	T	W	T	F	S
1	2	3	4	5	6	7
8	9	10	11	12	13	14
15	16	17	18	19	20	21
22	23	24	25	26	27	28
29	30					

JULY
S	M	T	W	T	F	S
		1	2	3	4	5
6	7	8	9	10	11	12
13	14	15	16	17	18	19
20	21	22	23	24	25	26
27	28	29	30	31		

AUGUST
S	M	T	W	T	F	S
					1	2
3	4	5	6	7	8	9
10	11	12	13	14	15	16
17	18	19	20	21	22	23
24	25	26	27	28	29	30
31						

SEPTEMBER
S	M	T	W	T	F	S
	1	2	3	4	5	6
7	8	9	10	11	12	13
14	15	16	17	18	19	20
21	22	23	24	25	26	27
28	29	30				

OCTOBER
S	M	T	W	T	F	S
			1	2	3	4
5	6	7	8	9	10	11
12	13	14	15	16	17	18
19	20	21	22	23	24	25
26	27	28	29	30	31	

NOVEMBER
S	M	T	W	T	F	S
						1
2	3	4	5	6	7	8
9	10	11	12	13	14	15
16	17	18	19	20	21	22
23	24	25	26	27	28	29
30						

DECEMBER
S	M	T	W	T	F	S
	1	2	3	4	5	6
7	8	9	10	11	12	13
14	15	16	17	18	19	20
21	22	23	24	25	26	27
28	29	30	31			

2026

JANUARY
S	M	T	W	T	F	S
				1	2	3
4	5	6	7	8	9	10
11	12	13	14	15	16	17
18	19	20	21	22	23	24
25	26	27	28	29	30	31

FEBRUARY
S	M	T	W	T	F	S
1	2	3	4	5	6	7
8	9	10	11	12	13	14
15	16	17	18	19	20	21
22	23	24	25	26	27	28

MARCH
S	M	T	W	T	F	S
1	2	3	4	5	6	7
8	9	10	11	12	13	14
15	16	17	18	19	20	21
22	23	24	25	26	27	28
29	30	31				

APRIL
S	M	T	W	T	F	S
			1	2	3	4
5	6	7	8	9	10	11
12	13	14	15	16	17	18
19	20	21	22	23	24	25
26	27	28	29	30		

MAY
S	M	T	W	T	F	S
					1	2
3	4	5	6	7	8	9
10	11	12	13	14	15	16
17	18	19	20	21	22	23
24	25	26	27	28	29	30
31						

JUNE
S	M	T	W	T	F	S
	1	2	3	4	5	6
7	8	9	10	11	12	13
14	15	16	17	18	19	20
21	22	23	24	25	26	27
28	29	30				

JULY
S	M	T	W	T	F	S
			1	2	3	4
5	6	7	8	9	10	11
12	13	14	15	16	17	18
19	20	21	22	23	24	25
26	27	28	29	30	31	

AUGUST
S	M	T	W	T	F	S
						1
2	3	4	5	6	7	8
9	10	11	12	13	14	15
16	17	18	19	20	21	22
23	24	25	26	27	28	29
30	31					

SEPTEMBER
S	M	T	W	T	F	S
		1	2	3	4	5
6	7	8	9	10	11	12
13	14	15	16	17	18	19
20	21	22	23	24	25	26
27	28	29	30			

OCTOBER
S	M	T	W	T	F	S
				1	2	3
4	5	6	7	8	9	10
11	12	13	14	15	16	17
18	19	20	21	22	23	24
25	26	27	28	29	30	31

NOVEMBER
S	M	T	W	T	F	S
1	2	3	4	5	6	7
8	9	10	11	12	13	14
15	16	17	18	19	20	21
22	23	24	25	26	27	28
29	30					

DECEMBER
S	M	T	W	T	F	S
		1	2	3	4	5
6	7	8	9	10	11	12
13	14	15	16	17	18	19
20	21	22	23	24	25	26
27	28	29	30	31